We've Gotta Reach Em' To Teach Em'

Where Teaching Intersects the Human Condition

Homeless teens from Traverse City, Michigan whom we invited to be an integral part of our graduate class entitled "Pop Culture Pedagogy".

By:
Dr. Elizabeth Johnson
Mary Kathleen Walsh

Published in 2006 by

Huron Valley Publishing, Inc.
4557 Washtenaw Avenue
Ann Arbor, Michigan 48108
(734) 971-2135
(800) PRINT-01
E-Mail: publish@hvpi.com
Website: www.hvpi.com

ISBN: 1-933377-09-7

Table of Contents

Dedication

When the going gets tough, life gets tougher and requires fervent help and support from those whom you are most deeply connected too—that is our families and our faith. First of all, we both married our precious gentlemen—gentle men who came into our lives while we were teenagers. They have been an integral part of our educational and personal pursuits and are our greatest cheerleaders as well as our most astute critics. We love you both profoundly and look forward to continuing to spend a lifetime with you! Thank you S.T. and Tim for being the men that have *loved so miraculously* and *given so freely* . . . AND for hanging in there when we stated 500 times that, "Hey . . . we are almost done!"

To our dear children and families:
<u>Elizabeth's</u>

This book is also dedicated to the "other" men in my life as well as to two very special women. First . . . to my 4 sons . . . S.T. III, Jeff, Greg, and Charles Johnson . . . Well guys, the book is finally written and published! Hooray! Thank you for allowing me the opportunity to experience the wild rollercoaster that evidenced 5 men and 1 woman in a home at one time! I consider it pure joy to have been called to be your mom. You have been patient with me as I have grown up and you all continue to be my greatest reason for celebrating life! To my father, Al Alley . . . Daddy, thank you for working long hours in order to send me to college and for believing in my potential! Like you, I miss mother (Virginia), especially the many years that I listened and watched her teach kindergarten. This book has been written with her humor and extreme sassiness in mind! To my daughter-in-law Jenny, who is a dynamic high school English teacher and a stellar mother to my grandson, S.T. Johnson, IV! Lastly, to S.T. IV (a.k.a. Tigger) . . . may this book serve as a legacy to you about what I believe to be one of the greatest callings . . . that of teaching. I love you with all of my heart and can't wait to see how you, too, will make a critical difference and affect lives for an eternity!

Kathy's

Thank you to my children Shannon and Michael Walsh for teaching me what it really means to love and be loved. You've taught me patience and have given me a reason to live in this crazy world. If it weren't for you, I would not be who I am today. To my parents Carol and Wally, whom I love deeply. Thank you for all your support and for believing in me and encouraging me never to give up. To Nancy, who has inspired me with her own innovative teaching style. For my grandmother, Martha Gough, who introduced me to the greatest calling in the world and who helped me realize my love for teaching. For my sisters, Suzy and Kelley, who have given me unending support and love in all facets of my life! I love you both very much. This dedication would never be right without a special thanks to my mentor and dear friend Elizabeth, whom I will be forever grateful! Thank you for all of the doors you opened for me during my journey into the greatest calling in the world. You have helped illuminate the world of teaching for me, from dream to reality; believing in my style beyond what even I perceived possible. You have helped me work outside the box into a world I always hoped to go. You will never know how much I appreciate you. I love you my friend!

We extend this dedication to Caribou Coffee in New Hudson, Michigan and Java House in South Lyon, Michigan and to Marriot Eagle Crest in Ypsilanti, Michigan, for the many hours we sat drinking coffee, utilizing electricity and for the unbelievable hospitality given to us as we wrote this book. You will forever have our patronage. Thank you very much!

"Their hearts were fired . . . their thoughts driven by a dream about their own classroom of students. That dream possessed them, and imperiously ruled over their minds and shaped their destinies, compelling them to go forth on what many called a 'fool's errand'. For it was on a fool's errand upon which they began their journey . . . a call to make a difference in this very difficult world. In a sense, they were casting their fishing nets into a sea—a turbulent human sea with children's souls held captive by pain, hopelessness, and rejection. You see, teaching is a fervent call that ignites the soul and summons the heart. It's mission . . . to eliminate pain and engender hope and joy within a generation held in bondage by an abyss of rejection."

Chapter ½
"Taking the First Step"

Colleagues, it is with great excitement that we begin our quest into reclaiming joy. The dance of joy is like no other; it's a dance whose melody and beat originate from our heart; whose choreography ignite our deepest of emotions; whose stage is our classroom; whose audience, our students and the families that love them profoundly. The dance of joy requires a lifetime of continued practice accompanied by many failed performances. As pedagogical artists, we are on stage both in and out of school. Reclaiming joy is an adventure that many are unwilling to embark upon or invest in. Why would one *not* choose joy? Sadly, many crave joy, yet have not been given the necessary tools or mentoring. Yes, joy is a choice! The fact is that we cannot always control what happens within our lives, but we can choose how to walk through it. It requires that we must first deal directly with our pain, desperation, frustration, emptiness, severed relationships, biases, selfishness, fear, and rejection. This is not a self-help book, but a help-self plea designed for educators to revisit and reconnect with their life's purpose and calling. It is a journey of contemplation, restoration, and abundant celebration. For some readers, our words will SHOUT affirmation and edification . . . for others, though; our words may serve as enigmatic proclamations.

Chapter 1 invites educators to journey into the uncharted sector of one's heart. This chapter illuminates *our* personal reflections as well as a critical examination of what we believe is the current state of the heart of education. We ask that you bear with us within the first several pages in that we allowed our hearts to figuratively state our literal experiences. Throughout our book we often use figurative language because we could not adequately express our true emotions within the confines of the literal. Interestingly enough, when one has totally exhausted their plethora of literal words driven by the head, the heart takes over and journeys within the endless boundaries of the figurative. You see, the figurative begins where the literal ends! The first several pages are a declaration of what we believe about education. Following these beginning pages, our ideas, thoughts, and feelings are more traditionally spoken.

Chapter 2 graphically exposes *life's* Pandora's Box and in doing so, discloses how pain can be of the forefront of predicting one's purpose and key to unlocking the meaning of life. We will reveal how pain is *no respecter of persons* and how unrelenting pain may be the greatest explorer of a human life. Opening Pandora's Box reopens the deepest of wounds that are exposed within the human heart. This chapter culminates in unfolding and illuminating our most pressing moral mandate as teachers. Clearly we believe wholeheartedly in the old cliché which broadcasts, "No pain, no gain"! Stay tuned . . .

When constructing Chapter 3, we realized that it would have to be one that examined the stumbling blocks inherent in discovering our purpose. We articulate and reveal how negativity and self-obsession are two volatile purpose-destroyers. Our true life purpose will be miraculously revealed *only* when we assertively cleanse ourselves of selfishness and our obsession with worldly successes.

Chapter 4 acknowledges the monumental gap between school-smart and street-smart. It seeks to unite the two polar entities by utilizing pop culture as its mighty bridge. This chapter heralds and continues to support the premise that education superimposed, void of the human experience, is morally wrong. Pop culture is all about human experience! Within the context of this very practical chapter, we identify extreme reach em' to teach em' instructional strategies that have the potential to greatly increase student achievement, aid in closing the achievement gap, as well as rekindling outrageous joy.

Lastly, Chapter 5 positions the teacher as a powerful superhero within the life of a child. It dispels the myth that a superhero's arsenal of powers are only skin deep. A real superhero,

one that our students and families can get their arms around, is the
not-so-super Superman. ***Teaching is heroism rooted in the heart
not the biceps.***

Now, let's embark upon a journey into reclaiming/claiming
our purpose toward affecting the lives of students and staff for
an eternity. In doing so, we can again experience the intense
excitement, joy, exuberance, deep intentions, and all that it was
cracked-up to be when we first answered our glorious call to teach.
Let's now re-enroll in a simple dance class—one that is aimed at
perfecting life's vibrant dance of joy. You see, embarking upon
any monumental adventure, including choreographing the dance
of joy, begins with conceiving and taking the first step. Ready
. . . 5-6-7-8

Chapter 1
"The Lost Life of the Heart"

*After endless years of feeding on lifeless curriculum,
endless performance standards, and unyielding pedagogy,
a jilted mind and thirsty heart will eventually
reach a cognitive desert
and will die a lonely death in the classroom.*

After many years into our educational journey as teachers, after the great waves of anticipation that marked the beginning of our pilgrimage have begun to ebb into life's middle years of service, there exists a still, diminutive voice awaiting to be summoned. This voice seeks entrance into what we will call the heart's *place of further still*. This uncharted sector allows one to explore the hidden questions of the heart which are fashioned out of one's intimate stories and experiences.

This voice churning inside the centrality of the heart begins its development as a fleeting thought. It can be likened to cheap perfume; it quickly emits a lustful scent that attracts the mind's attention, yet immediately the fragrance is adulterated and seemingly lost. In infancy, this voice is dismissed as imaginary and unfounded. Yet, over time, it grows into an articulated message that craftfully finds its way into the defenseless thoughts of the mind. Finally, this message permeates the *place of further still* in vulnerable moments in which the core of our heart is most unedited.

The afterbirth is an engendered language. The storied narratives that ignite each beat, creates a penetrating symphony of passions, dreams, fears, and the deepest of wounds. This intimate place does not respond to harsh principles, state mandates, reform efforts, objectives, standardized tests or benchmarks. These potential life-destroying forces have not only assaulted the life-giving entities of the heart, they have raped its geographical transcendence. This private place doesn't thrive on efficiency, but romance, ecstasy, joy, adventure, and gallantry. This unfathomable place yearns for intimate relationships of heroic proportion. It is a magnificent dwelling of personal solitude where heroes and heroines are fashioned; resembling a mighty Mount Olympus or the heavens where angels are beckoned and marvelously equipped for service. It is a place where an ignited, fledgling teacher is called into a life's service. It is also an acute care center where exhausted and system-abused educators can retreat for renewal, reawakening, and recommitment. It is within this realm that this book has been conceived and birthed.

There has historically been a great debate as to what teaching *really* is all about. Is it a profession, a career, vocation, or blind adherence to what some perceive as a job perpetuating the myth called "summers off"? Is it possible that one selects *education* from the career vending machine because they have been led to believe that it is less rigorous? Many believe that teaching is a last-ditch alternative due to failure in more notorious (tongue-in-cheek) fields that are certainly believed to be more lucrative and intellectually stimulating. After all, teaching will not allow one to catapult the social status ladder and thereby fill a five-car garage with elite, European automobiles! Teaching is not a 6 figure job . . . but one with 25+ figures (in the classroom)! Haven't you heard the propaganda broadcasting, "Those who can't . . . teach!" Why do some fall victim to blindly purchasing these false-bill-of-goods? Some hypothesize that one selects teaching simply because their mother or father was a teacher. Is it such a reprehensible transgression to walk in the footprints of giants? How many individuals select business due to the influence of other family members? Lastly, if teaching *was* a choice, why would anyone really choose to pursue a teaching degree in light of the interminable unrest holding the field of education hostage? Why teaching? Why now? Why anytime?

Teaching is *not* something one pursues in light of continued failed attempts at other careers that the world believes are more rigorous and respectable; although it can appear to happen in this manner. Teaching was never wrought to be cast as an illegitimate child at a family reunion or as an add-on within any entity. Teaching is a separate and distinct organic force and out-of-it manifests the breath of life. Teaching is not dead or able to be inorganically-manufactured. Sadly, some aspects of education are being commandeered by dead curriculum and by those who have lost their vision. Some advocate that pedagogy can be artificially inseminated and cloned! It appears that the ***art of teaching*** has been cast within a dark tomb and its life force must be resurrected and recast within its proper dimension.

Allow us to fervently state with no apologies or reservations, that teaching is not a choice . . . a profession . . . and certainly not a career. Furthermore, it is not an afterthought or aftermath. The art of teaching, the essence of learning as well as the ensuing, courageous expedition, is like no other. Secondary to parenting, teaching sets the heroic bar for preparing young and older minds to affect generations for an eternity. Teaching is the great choreographer of life.

The ***call to teach*** can certainly come after a financially successful, yet thoroughly emotionally-unfulfilling career. It is incredible to witness how many highly, h i g h l y successful business folks abandon the world's definition of "success" to return to higher education for teacher certification. These awakened individuals are quick to confess that the lucrative money, travel, expense account, and car were lonely perks that gathered dust and moths within their hearts. Therefore, the seeds of teaching do not ***only*** take root when one is young; rather, they can take root at any period within one's life, even as early as 90 years old! These seeds, if implanted and fertilized, will eventually grow and magnify into an incessant, parasitic command, cultivated within one's heart and soul. Much like an obnoxious parasite, teaching first begins with a minute infestation and multiplies into a powerful take-over. The result is a heart and soul that elicits a white flag of surrender and a maddening declaration of teaching as their vibrant calling worthy of endless preparation and pain.

Drum role please . . .

Teaching HAS, IS, and WILL ALWAYS be a calling—
a spiritual summons to endure years of treacherous
terrain, unbearable climates, endless high-peaked
mountains, unyielding quicksand, and frightening
fissures. Teaching is a miraculous stewardship. It is
within this act of stewardship where the intersection of
pain and joy unite and unconditional love abounds.

Our interest in writing this book is more than professional,
it's profoundly personal. Our book is suggestive, not exhaustive.
For that reason, we have decided to publish it ourselves to ensure
that an editor doesn't alter our words and deep intentions. Prior to
reading our work and words, know that our combined 47 years of
teaching and administrative experience and a combined 50 years of
parenting, penetrate every thought, word, and idea throughout. As
a professor and president of an educational consulting company,
we continue to provide extensive professional development to
teachers, administrators, and parents all over the United States. We
have teamed up as educational consultants to provide services to
schools in radically diverse demographic areas and populations.

As consultants, we take on many roles and responsibilities
with regard to servicing the professional development needs of
a school district. We begin our work within a school/district by
conducting a thorough needs assessment and intense interviews
with administrators and staff. We align the assessment to the
criteria that is articulated by the accrediting agency selected by the
district. Certainly, many of our schools work closely with North
Central Association Commission of Accreditation and School
Improvement (NCA CASI). This non-governmental, voluntary
organization offers accreditation to over 9,000 public and private
schools within 19 states. NCA also offers accreditation to the
Navajo Nation and the Department of Defense Dependent's

Schools worldwide. We continue to conduct workshops for NCA's individual teaching and assessment conferences held locally and nationally.

Following data analysis from the needs assessment, we construct an individualized, strategic action plan with regard to a district's curriculum, instruction, and assessment ventures. Alongside district personnel, we assist in carving-out both a vision and plan-of-attack to help them accomplish their stated outcomes. Lastly, we create and provide the necessary workshops, seminars, and a follow-up strategic plan to ***shut-the-dam*** on the achievement gulf! Working with these schools is an intriguing and invigorating adventure! It is so thrilling to come-along-side these caring educators whose foremost mission is servicing families and the children who grace their classrooms.

Many times, while working with a particular district, we are asked to come-on-board with individual schools and work intimately with their parent organizations. After all, parents hold the key to the frustration box of a child! DUUH . . . a shocking revelation! Our most cherished moments have been spent, drinking endless amounts of coffee (and sugar-infested Hi C juice), with parents who are officers within their respective parent organizations. We realized very quickly that when we come together as parents, our deep connection and vision for our children transcends our individual education, socio-economic means, culture, experiences, personal biases, and our privilege or lack of it. The sharing of our struggles, frustrations, fears, and stories that illuminate our deep pain accompanying child-rearing, sews the common thread that unites us as extreme advocates for our kids. The power of seeing the tears within each of our eyes as we speak of our struggles, provide the impetus for uniting for the cause of ALL children rather than just focusing upon our own babies exclusively.

*After all, it takes many parents to raise a child—or
more profoundly, it takes a struggling child to illuminate
the human frailty within a parent. Admittedly, it is within
our own vulnerability as parents that our humility is
miraculously unearthed! Clearly, pain is no respecter
of persons and possesses no inhibitions and limitations.
Pain engenders equity.*

Furthermore, we have the unique privilege of serving
educators and parents within a multiplicity of private, religious,
and public school settings. One week you might see us in the
"poorest of the poor" schools in the Midwest; the next week in
Native schools throughout the Western and Southwestern states
and eventually making our way to serve elite schools out East.
We continue to receive "Code Blue" calls from system-fatigued
principals and central office administrators from every part of our
nation looking for a sure-fire cure to restore joy and hope within
their respective building/district. We hear their reverberations
regarding the system and acknowledge their unyielding dedication
to their staff, families, and students.
While working intimately with schools, their dynamic
administrators and teachers, we continue to witness a malaise; an
alarming evolutionary *discourse of hopelessness* among teachers,
parents, and principals as well in many of the students. As we move
through the many classrooms and have candid conversations with
dedicated educators, we see those we serve in deep, deep pain and
frustration. Each tries with great diligence to deconstruct the ways
and means as to how to meet mandates and still reach and teach all
children. Are state mandates and the realities of classroom teaching
really meant to be such polar entities and enemies? In the minds
of many educators, mandates are not on their short list, given the
bleak *state of the heart* of many of their students! It should not be
shocking that many educators are still trying to figure out how to
get kids to attend school on a daily basis. It's simply unethical to

expect teachers to fully ***sell-out*** to mandates and the performance-based testing that has been bought and sold as the ***be-all-and-end-all*** when so many of their students are emotionally distraught.

We hear and acknowledge the cries from staff who reveal an alarming increase in students whose lives are entangled within the deep and dark abyss of depression and despair! As staff developers, we are privy to their inhumane pain, frustration, and exhaustion that they endure. Adults who enter a school including many parents, tutors, student teachers, and other visitors, have virtually ***no-clue*** as to the desperation and silent suffering that staff and students endure. Interestingly enough, many will exit a school totally oblivious of the emotional and exacerbating malignancy growing within the hearts of those who try to cope. We wholeheartedly believe in ***educator accountability.*** Every educator must account-for and be accountable-to those they serve. We MUST align curriculum, instruction, and assessment to developmentally-appropriate standards, outcomes, and assessments. (Note: We believe that the term ***developmentally-appropriate*** does not end in kindergarten or first grade, but is a living, breathing epistemological mindset that should permeate all levels, including post-doctoral!) Developmental appropriateness is at the forefront of differentiation of instruction. Differentiation is the scaffolding upon which to build an equity-driven pedagogy. Teaching for equity is the cornerstone of multicultural/multiethnic education. Multicultural education is the dynamic lens upon which to examine the human condition (the joy as well as the pain inherent within the soul of humanity). Teaching to the human condition IS our work—our mission—our journey—our heart--our purpose.

Furthermore, we acknowledge that outcomes, benchmarks, standards, grade level content expectations, assessments, and AYP have validity, yet must be weighed, measured, and enforced in light of a student's experience and within the fragility of their

emotional state. We unequivocally believe that teachers deeply desire to teach within the intersection where content delivery meets the human condition (a novel concept).

In trying to pull off this feat of madness, a teacher will encounter students who are *academically far behind* juxtaposed with *academically far exceeding* mandates that serve as the great enforcer of *quick* mastery. This deadly combination yields quantitative hysteria and an inhumane paradox. This paradoxical feat (*academically far behind students measured by academically far exceeding mandates void of the human condition*) is much like moving the Barnum & Bailey Circus from New York to Hong Kong in a 10 foot aluminum boat with a Level 5 hurricane on the horizon! Yes, there are some animals that have a chance to swim or tread water and have some possibility to reach the shore or be rescued. Why? Because they have had the privilege of learning how to swim under the most ominous conditions. Others, however, cannot endure the insurmountable waves, salt water, sharks, and in exhaustion, will succumb and drown. The rescue efforts to reach these animals would be in vain due to their inability to swim. Why? Because these animals have been wounded, underfed, homeless and without an advocate/trainer.

Educators genuinely *seek-to-understand*, yet sincerely ask, "Why do theses mandates position our teachers and students within lose-lose situations?" Candidly, they demand an answer to the question, "Why are so many of our district-driven student assessments, grade level expectations, and timeframes totally oblivious to the challenges ever present within each student, family, and classroom community?" Teachers have zero problems with high expectations and zero tolerance for unethical and inappropriate practices. Seeking an answer to this question is NOT meant to engender educator excuses for poor student academic achievement. It is meant to begin candid conversations within each school staff meeting and school board meeting. We acknowledge this dilemma and wholeheartedly believe that the achievement gap IS this paradox.

We have been invited to sit with faculty as their principals announced the results of their state assessment scores. Our role within these meetings is to offer collegial support and hope to the staff after the dismal results are announced. We witness how the merit of teachers and their students are judged in light of a few quantitative scores. How would you like to have your life's work showcased using a single score or set of scores? The data that are really the most relevant are the qualitative data, the "rest of the story" if you will, about each child. These data rarely enter into the equation for judging teacher effectiveness and the accompanying student achievement/potential. These contextual types of data are viewed, many times, as punitive and have little or no bearing on the single scores that are publicly reported. Yet, these data fall on barren, clay ground as far as the media and *powers-to-be* are concerned! The final score is the final verdict regarding the merit of a teacher, their students, as well as the validity of an individual school! To measure the integrity of a teacher and academic potential of a student on a few test scores is inhumane! Clearly, teachers have penetrating questions and deep concerns. Their deep concerns are endless and mandated solutions seemingly mindless.

The most critical, penetrating question that many of our teachers inwardly ask is, "Why am I losing my passion for teaching and patience with my principal, parents, and colleagues?" Colleagues, why is this type of *silenced inquiry* becoming the rule rather than the exception? After all, as educators, we are told to *fear not* because the educational messiah is finally here wearing the white robe of righteousness engraven with the letters "NCLB"! Is this phenomenon really the educational messiah or the educational adversary on the horizon? Are the mandates and their accompanying "Catch 22" assessments packaged and marketed as the *be-all-and-end-all* remedy for every educational disease? We believe wholeheartedly that those who drive policy have excellent intentions and deeply care for kids and families, yet how many of them are immersed within the trenches of teaching? After all, it's easier to dictate on benches than work tirelessly in trenches!

To be fair, we do evidence exciting pockets of vibrant learning within many, m a n y schools. Our schools are **bursting at the seams** with countless educators whose hearts are **on-fire** for the kids. Consistently, this exuberance is found in educators who are able to withstand brutal attacks. We believe that their ability to persevere, given extreme battle fatigue, is due to a fervent embracing of a life purpose and a personal vision for those they humbly serve. They have not fallen victim to "administrivia". These educators **do what they have to do** and are not deterred by wavering bureaucratic demands and finger-pointing that attempts to rape their pedagogy, malign their exceedingly high expectations, and steal their joy. These individuals use best practice strategies to **ignite and excite** as well as proactive, compassionate classroom management to **engender student internal accountability and corporate community.** We applaud their inner core of strength and purposeful life that creates a mighty fortress against those forces that seek to conquer and destroy!

The heartrending classroom realities that we witness almost daily are teachers who are driven and forced to **cover** truckloads of content (some of which are mindless, disconnected facts). They have fallen victim to the **content-rat-race** that takes place within a suicidal maze void of escape routes! On many occasions we hear our colleagues' herald, "I only have 15 weeks to cover 20 chapters!" There exasperation may be due to the tremendous unrealistic demands placed upon them. They feel like they can no longer be creative "curriculum designers" but are now forced to become rabid "curriculum consumers". Therefore, we witness a continued rigid, directed instruction (lecture with zero active student engagement) that generates boredom and even lower student achievement. This force-fed, Atkins-compliant pedagogical buffet serves "all the facts you can eat and test questions that you can regurgitate". This color-in-the-right-response, reductionist construct has manifested into an educational abyss perpetuated by a developmentally-inappropriate, mandated psychosis. Our educators are held under a tyranny that seeks to reduce our students to a cognitively-starved, bulimic state in compliance with "No Digestive Tract Left Behind"!

Interestingly enough, we have ***never*** been in a school that was completely free from these dilemmas and painful exasperation. We hear their war stories whose plots are set within the contexts of both private and public settings. Clearly, we all came over in different educational ships, but now, we are all in the same bureaucratic boat (the Titanic with its lurking, hidden icebergs)! To sum it all up, allow us to make the following declaration:

Every teacher, parent, student, and administrator that we have met, regardless of their fervent passion and exhaustive dedication, acknowledges a thirst for a massive dose of joy! Restoring joy in educators and parents is the reason why we are writing this book. Clearly, WE LOVE WHAT WE DO and DO WHAT WE LOVE!

Lastly, many great teachers are working diligently to assist in raising our nation's youth. They are to be heralded and protected from those whose fiery darts seek to penetrate and kill their spirit. Each day, they are in the fox holes fighting diligently for equity, freedom, and for disarming the Tsunami (achievement gap). We all can certainly attest to several teachers who *fight the fight*! Yet, hidden behind the walls of humility, exists a small handful of teachers found at the intersection where content meets the human condition. These gentle giants are a part of, what we will call the top 2% of teachers whose world and work are so far beyond any literal or figurative interpretation! There are no words that can accurately display the power of their person. These individuals have moved from a call to teach, to the heralding cry of *humanitarian* (a call within a call)! We salute them and stand in awe of their *art* and humbled by their contagious compassion for serving the "weakest of the weak"—that is, our nation's severely marginalized youth and families.

These icons have catapulted racial, economic, social, and religious barriers and have given no air time to being "politically correct". They never assimilated into traditional societal templates or rigid gender constructs. Most have taught under the most atrocious conditions and sought peace and joy when others were quitting, argumentative, and on a major *poor-me* party. In fact, when confronted with a continuous regiment of impossibilities, their zeal and passion for kids ignited even a greater inferno and fervor within their hearts. Lastly, these *champions-for-the-cause* never compromised their ethical and moral walk. They quietly and simply did what they were called to do; that is, to fervently serve others in unbearable pain. These individuals can clearly articulate their purpose at any given time and place. We have looked to these educators as our crafting-mechanism for this book.

These humble colleagues of ours are the heroes and heroines who help students carve a vision and dream far beyond their sun-baked, hopeless horizons. They are the real superheroes whose powers disarm every villain. Their mighty weapon . . . a simple piece of chalk. Their writings and words . . . weighty and strong. Their personal presence is rather unimposing. They are not ostentatious or showy. Their motto is rather simple, "Whatever It Takes!" Their transparent humanity, genuine humility, and absolute honesty engender their greatest testimony and witness. Honesty possesses a beautiful and refreshing simplicity, doesn't it? They possess no hidden agendas, hypocrisy, political games, or dog and pony shows. They are completely *sold-out* to kids and families. Their model for servanthood will expose the fake and destroy the artificial. These freedom fighters, true humanitarians, and social activists are dream-sustainers for students and families whose life portraits have a thick, diagonal red line crossed through them. As you make your journey through the book, it is our fervent hope that you can draw strength as well as a powerful provision to rethink and retool what it means to teach and reach.

Sometimes, it is necessary to unlearn by burying our old, predictable tapes and peacefully rebelling against contentment. Remember, in order for you to know where you are from, you must leave. Many times it takes an act of personal pedagogical mutiny to muster up an outrageous universe of alternatives that can unfetter our ingenuity. After all, a dark, dreary, and rugged cocoon that survives the elements has the potential to metamorphose into a beautiful butterfly that moves majestically while entreating every eye it rests upon!

Colleagues, we are called to be contemplatives in the midst of our very complex world. A contemplative is one who possesses a transformative presence in the life of students, families, and colleagues. A contemplative, in the heart of our challenging world, doesn't retreat to desert places or desolate islands. Active and contemplative do not exist within two different dominions. Contemplation is in the action, in the very process. Active and contemplative are not two different lives that an educator leads. Contemplation is a rigorous reflective tool that, when it reaches a given level of intensity, spreads its surplus into action. If action is to be abundant, it must be marinated in calculated reflection. Action and contemplation should always bring one back to the *act of zealous serving*. Remember; the greatest of teachers vibrantly serve those who follow them!

May our work and words unleash the power of your genius toward working unceasingly and unselfishly for the cause of kids and the families that love them profoundly.

Chapter 2
"*Opening Pandora's Box*"

In the incredible fantasy book, **Tuck Everlasting**, Winnie Foster is faced with a decision of a lifetime; one that has the potential to rewrite her destiny. She is given the opportunity to live forever by drinking magical water from an immortal spring. This dilemma *is* the figurative protagonist; the uncompromising, lucrative duality created by author Natalie Babbit. Will Winnie choose the fountain of youth by drinking from the spring of everlasting life or yield to a predestined life manicured in the way that nature majestically contrived it to be? In other words, will she select the path conjured up by nature or compromise her destiny by reconstructing her eternity? This duality is not far-fetched and parallels the enticements that our youth and many adults struggle with. Face it, wouldn't we all trample over each other in a fanatical frenzy toward purchasing bottles of this magical water! Don't you think people would stand in endless lines and offer exorbitant amounts of the "green stuff" just to purchase even a small eyedropper of this wondrous liquid? Let's not forget the long lines that our grandparents stood in just to receive the flu vaccine that was in such short supply! Oh, that wonderful "supply and demand" concept is an emotional enticement in and of itself, isn't it?

A critical analysis of this wonderful novel might expose a dilemma (Pandora's Box) yet to be unearthed/opened. The story takes place within a small town called Treegap located in the foothills of the Adirondack Mountains. Winnie is a spunky girl with wealthy, seemingly emotionally detached parents. Her parents seek to disarm her heart and head and place her within the confines of a territorial fence. She defies them by running away and is internally driven to explore the forest and its magnificent mystique. She meets and falls in love with a young man named Jessie Tuck who eventually discloses that he and his family will live forever because they drank from a fountain of immortality. He offers Winnie the same opportunity and she is torn between the personal choice of living an eternal physical life or yielding to an eventual corporeal death orchestrated by nature. The Tuck Family opens Pandora's paradoxical box by disclosing the truth inherent in human frailty as well as the consequences of choosing human immortality. This duality tantalizes and never compromises.

Winnie is left with a monumental decision; one that seeks to alter her human cycle. Why is she so torn? On the surface it seems like such a no-brainer decision; who wouldn't want to live forever? Yet, her head, heart, and soul are a turbulent trinity seeking solace. Many questions arise as she is held captive by this trilogy. These are questions that even the most astute critics of this novel attempt to answer. "Why did the mystique of the forest powerfully penetrate her vulnerabilities? What was Winnie's conception of life and death? Did she possess any understanding of the meaning of life? How can a young girl comprehend mortality and better yet, immortality? What decision would each of us make if placed within this paradoxical and poisonous fountain of youth? Colleagues, what *wheel of misfortune* might you spin—human immortality or corporeal death? What decision *did* she make? Ahhh . . . the plot and the forest thickens!

Reintroducing the provocative concept called PURPOSE. This is a captivating word that has been a part of our essence since our conception. Purpose WAS, IS and ALWAYS WILL be a viable topic for human interaction and consumption. For centuries philosophers have attempted to prod and probe critical questions permeating our vast human experience. Secondary to the age old question, "What is truth?", lays the second most exhilarating rhetorical inquiry. For thousands of years the most *profound of the profound* have pondered the question, "What is the meaning of life?" Hugh S. Moorhead, university philosophy professor, attempted to answer that question by querying 250 of the most prominent minds in the world. The list of intellects he asked included auspicious philosophers, scientists, and literary geniuses. His 1998 publication entitled, *The Meaning of Life According to*

Our Century's Greatest Writers and Thinkers, chronicles their answers.

Their responses to this question could be cast within three different perspectives. First, several intellectual giants put forth their best guesses with seemingly great frustration in constructing their responses. The second set of replies included tongue-in-cheek confessions that they had ***made-up*** a purpose for life. The third group was brutally honest in their admissions that they were totally clueless! Interestingly enough, many of these intellects eventually wrote to Professor Moorhead and asked him if ***he*** had come to any conclusions regarding the meaning of life! Say what? These findings leave us with even a more embalming question. Given the fact that our world's extraordinary minds are held hostage by this sobering question, is it ***really*** feasible for common folks to define, discover, and embrace the meaning of life? Can those who appear to be rather ordinary and lead a seemingly simple life, define that which is considered complex? Interesting question, huh? Let's move on . . .

There are many, many other famous individuals that also have floundered to uncover the meaning of life and offer a unique definition of purpose. Carl Jung, world-renowned psychiatrist states, "I don't know the meaning, the purpose of life, but it looks as if something was meant by it." Hey Carl . . . you are supposed to have an answer to life--what's up with that brother? Now let's consider the infamous Isaac Asimov, scientist and science fiction writer. He reports, "As far as I can see, there is no purpose." Wow, Isaac that was really profound! What a scary thought! Lastly, let's query the intriguing pop culture icon . . . Rap artist, Ice T! An analysis of one of his song lyrics clearly reveals what he might hold as the essence of life. He sings, ***"The only reason we're here is to reproduce. Just chill out and reproduce. Keep the species alive!"*** Yo, Mr. Ice T, you may want to change to another beverage to quench your thirst for a meaning in life! Imagine living your life as a tea bag whose total existence is a reliance on hot water!

Many individuals celebrate and find meaning in life

according to the standard called ***the amount of stuff*** or materialist goods that they can muster-up. The materialist, who is all about STUFF, believes that the purpose of life is to horde goods. Their essence of life is to ***out-do, re-do, can-do, have-to, should do, can't do, and must do!*** In other words, the quantity and quality of life is measured by what you have and own. More is better. Less in life is nothing to confess! Our question to the materialist is, "How many times have you ever seen a hearse, while on its way to the cemetery, stop and attach a trailer full of the dead man's possessions? Imagine if our life's meaning and purpose were measured by our ***pile of stuff***. Did you know that one of the fastest growing businesses is that of personal storage space? In other words, when our home overflows with stuff, we can rent a storage area to accommodate the excess! What a comforting thought; what an innovative invention. NOT! What is even more revealing is how our stuff is a tell-tale sign of what we value in life. A wise older friend once told us that a person's checkbook is a living tribute to what their life purpose is. Money infers meaning! Is it really possible that we can predict one's life purpose based upon the specific goods that we hold so dear to our heart? Scary thought! Time to have a garage sale! Is there no one out there who GETS it?

Internationally renowned psychiatrist Viktor E. Frankl published his masterwork, ***Man's Search for Meaning***, to purport his theory that man's life long destiny is to discover his innermost purpose and meaning. When asked about the tremendous success of his bestseller he reported, " . . . if hundreds of thousands of people reach out for a book whose very title promises to deal with the question of a meaning to life, it must be a question that burns under their fingernails." Interestingly enough, his text has evidenced its seventy-third printing in English as well as been translated in nineteen other languages. His disturbing essay unveils the torturous realities of a concentration camp. With wisdom and brutal remembrance as his compass and rudder, Frankl unveils a timeless, monumental proclamation. He declares that after every essence of a man is obliterated, including his aspirations and human freedom, he still possesses the ability to ***choose his attitude when given a unique set of circumstances***. Furthermore, he writes, "Ultimately, many should not ask what the meaning of his life is, but rather must recognize that it is ***he*** who is asked. In a word, each man is questioned by life; and he can only answer to life by answering for his own life; to life he can only respond by being responsible".

This brilliant Holocaust survivor clearly ***gets*** it! While imprisoned in a Nazi war camp, he observed that, while some just gave up and died, others remained positive. What made the difference? His conclusion was that it all depended on whether people had anything to live for such as a family they desired to see again. They certainly didn't choose life because of the materialistic goods they left behind! When you see and smell death, a sleek European car and gold VISA card is meaningless! Frankel ascertained that those with no purpose gave up and died. In other words, "What's the point if there is no point"? Frankel died in 1997 at the age of 92. What a great man! May his healing messages of truth abound. May the channels between our congested ears be unclogged to hear.

One of the most insightful writings about meaning and purpose that give the heart a wake-up call is ***The Velveteen Rabbit***, by Margery Williams. Let's take a brief moment and journey back to this riveting story; one that can be linked to every struggling student who graces our classrooms. It is a passionate portrayal; the core of humanity's cry for unconditional love. The following are excerpts that express the tenor of the book.

Once upon a time . . . "THERE WAS ONCE A VELVETEEN RABBIT, AND IN THE BEGIN-ning he was really splendid. He was fat and bunchy, as a rabbit should be [He had been stuffed in a stocking and placed on the mantel for a young boy during the holiday season] . . . There were other things in the stocking . . . but the Rabbit was quite the best of all . . . For a long time he lived in the toy cupboard or on the nursery floor, and no one thought very much about him . . . the poor little Rabbit was made to feel himself very insignificant and commonplace

. . . 'What is REAL' asked the Rabbit one day . . . Real isn't how you are made, said the Skin Horse [his only friend]. [Skin Horse continues speaking] It's a thing that happens to you . . . When a child loves you for a long, long time, not just to play with, but REALLY loves you, then you become Real . . . "

This touching story tugs at the delicate heartstrings of its reader. Is this tale really a plea for uncovering the unadulterated meaning of life? Is the term **real** correlated to discovering meaning in one's life? Educators . . . are we real? Do we place children within our classroom cognitive cupboard and attempt to *just* teach them? How many Velveteen Rabbits do we have feeling gagged and bound, shackled to their desks with no one willing to place an investment within their lifetime? Do we have contagious compassion and an intellectual hunger for recognizing the duality inherent within this human condition? Or, are we immune from diagnosing the human frailty within our schools? Remember taking the petals off a flower one at a time and saying, "He loves me, he loves me not, he loves me . . . ? You see, that's the duality, the repetitive exercise in human frailty; the inner turmoil of conditional versus unconditional love. Let us continue.

We will now turn to a narrative writing by a young mother who admittedly grew into a parent. We sat with her for hours listening to her saga of raising her children, specifically a daughter who was diagnosed with bi-polar disorder. We didn't specifically ask her about her purpose, but requested that she summarize the experience with her challenging child. The following are excerpts from her taped interview.

"It is no secret that I had my first child at a young age. It was a bittersweet moment—one filled with joy and anxiety about the journey I was about to embark upon. The realness of being a mother really didn't hit me until I brought my daughter home. I so wanted to go to college, but I knew that it was out-of-the-picture at this time. I really wanted to be a teacher because I wanted to serve kids. I didn't realize as a parent, I was also a teacher, before I was actually a teacher! When you are a parent,

you are also a teacher—or should be!

The first two years of her life was amazing . . . she was happy and we laughed together. I loved having my daughter. What a blessing to me. We went for walks and did all those things a mommy and baby should do together. Then lightening struck and my content little girl became an angry monster. At age 2 she began her typical defiance with temper tantrums. It wasn't until she moved from her baby years into her toddler stage that I realized I had to move from mommy to parent.

The terrible twos turned into the horrible threes and this turned into the frustration fours and on and on. It never subsided. My world felt like it was coming to an end. I didn't understand how this could happen. My heart ached with pain. From the time I came to terms with my pregnancy, I knew that having THIS child was serious business. How was I going to figure it all out? This was going to be a challenge of a lifetime.

Because of my faith, I always took the attitude that I had been blessed with a child and I better do it right! Yet, my daughter's continual disobedience, anger and flying-off-the-handle at simple things, led me on a new journey and roller coaster that I never expected. I couldn't fathom what the heck was going on. I was young. I didn't feel like I could take on the world and I had not come from a large family to fall back upon--in fact, I was an only child. The reality was that as a new mom, I was a child, myself. I kept telling myself that giving up was not an option. I felt an extremely high level of accountability to try and figure it all out.

I couldn't quite understand this new mission and accountability only that the pain I was feeling for my child was unbearable. How does a teenage mom handle such an explosive child? Where and who can a young teen-mom cry out to for help with an irate child? I wasn't ready to be a parent—nobody is at that age. But, I had to make myself be a parent! The obstacles that I was faced with, were endless. I was constantly worried that she would eventually choose suicide or fall victim to drugs, alcohol, and pre-marital sex. I wondered if someday she might end up in prison. The nightmares affected me while I was awake as well as asleep. I had to pull myself together, fast! My mission was to help her find peace before she graduated from high school—that was my target. I had to have her at a certain place prior to her leaving home—I was on a mission!

Getting a handle on parenting and a sense of my role in the life of my child began to bring peace to the tornado that plagued her thoughts and heart. For some unknown reason, I was driven to take a lot of parenting classes, read self-help books, observe more mature parents, and seek professional psychiatric assistance. After therapy, medications, doctor visitations, and many misdiagnoses, she was finally diagnosed with bi-polar disorder. Giving me this diagnosis was only helpful to a point, but didn't promise that things would get better. What it did allow me to do was to trudge forward to discover ways to help her find this peace in her mind; if that was even possible.

When I look back on it all, I know that I had been driven. I always felt that it was my job as a parent to prepare her to be productive and a contributing member of society. I can still remember having that as my goal as 'TEEN-MOM'! The love for my child drove me! Today, at age 27, she still struggles, but the demons that infest her emotions have drastically calmed down--but it is still a concern for me. This experience led me on a pursuit to find out more about struggling kids. I know that my story mimics many others. In closing, as the years have passed by, I have realized that her disorder has prepared me to reach children with similar struggles in a way no one else could. My journey allowed me to prepare the footprints upon which other parents can walk. You see, I am not 'all that' but one that did all-she-could-do! I'm just a parent who is a teacher without a degree!"

Go Mom, you had it going on girl! Colleagues, can you even imagine being a mother and a child, too? Leaping one giant step further, can you even fathom in that context, parenting an explosive child plagued with little or no peace within their fragile, disquieting mind? While listening attentively to her words, we were astonished as to her apparent gifts of wisdom and discernment at such a young age. After all, she had no role models or shining, stellar stars to latch her parent wagon onto. Her resources were limited as well as her financial base. After much reflection, we realized that this dynamic teen-mom was bountifully endowed with a disposition and insight conducive for parenting an exceptionally difficult daughter.

As we kept rehashing her interview, a mesmerizing question continued to permeate our thoughts? We kept asking, "How can a young teen with minimal experience babysitting, possess abilities that parallel a well-seasoned, mature parent?" We kept reading her narratives over and over again and finally realized that her story was certainly pregnant with hidden meaning waiting to be birthed. We looked for the themes of action and contemplation present within her words. Remember--these are the two acts of one who has a transformative presence and one who possesses the attributes of "zealous serving". We have come to the exciting conclusion that both she, and the mission that she was undertaking, had yielded a fertile breeding ground upon which to prepare her for a future unveiling of her purpose. May we be so bold as to hypothesize that her unrelenting tenacity for her child illuminated a predictor as to her eventual calling and purpose in life. Furthermore, she was clearly germinating the seeds of a humanitarian within her young, formative years. It was apparent that her complex child breathed life and meaning into her life. Her mature parenting experiences and decisions certainly unfolded the preparation for something very profound and sweet that would eventually take a deeper root (purpose) within her adult life. Lastly, if you carefully read her words, you noticed the phrase *"realness of being a mother didn't really hit me until I brought my daughter home"*. There's that word ***real*** again! This mother, like our precious Velveteen Rabbit, was about to realize that the art of becoming real is the unveiling of a sculpture affirming one's eventual purpose and meaning of life.

Colleagues, this excerpt from this dedicated mom evidences that even though, as a young teen, she couldn't speak forth an identified purpose, her actions spoke volumes. It is evident that this dedicated parent was led by her passion and inner gut to pursue intervention strategies for her daughter. How can a teenager have that much depth, breadth and be afforded such wisdom? Hmmmm—is it feasible that she was being prepared for something great and mighty once she had raised her daughter? Was there a call upon her life? Clearly, her actions were driven by rich meaning and purpose. For now, let us rest in the awareness that many times those who are called to serve may in fact be the immature, undereducated and the unskilled. Teaching/parenting does not call the equipped—it equips the called IF they possess a teachable and reachable heart much like the mom we just highlighted.

Allow us now to present a writing that transmits a rather different message; one shared from the journal entry written by an older teenager. Entrance into this narrative needs no triumphal entry or orchestrated prelude. What it does demand, is that the judge and jury, within the depths of our soul, declare a verdict upon those who hold guilt for this unpardonable human tragedy. All rise . . .

"Merky water beneath my soul,
Catapulting my heart beyond control.
Infesting the abyss of an insane mind,
With thoughts held captive, never to find.
Commanding, beckoning me to submerge,
An exhausted Soul disinclined to surge.
A quickened sand beneath my feet
Smothering, choking each mirror image it meets.
Everlasting demise to all who succumbs.
A shattered societal mirror forces me to run.
Religion taunting my belabored coffin
Teasing, torturing, accusatory sin
With no grace, or any room to bend.

**Discontinue life's disaster, which is me
With no advocate to speak my plea."**

Where does one go when they have virtually lost all meaning and purpose? Well, many go to school and sit within our classrooms and walk the halls of our schools. Many negotiate their day such that others are totally oblivious to the dark secrets that lurk within. Many parents are blinded and immune from sensing their depression and dismay. How do youth, whose lives are void of meaning and purpose, deal with the ***taunting, teasing, torturing, smothering, choking, exhausted and shattered*** "with no grace, or any room to bend"? The answer is very alarming and many do not really want to hear the harsh realities called the truth. To be perfectly honest, many of our young people (college students included), seek suicide, addiction, and bodily mutilation as their top ***outlets-of-choice*** for pain. We can't tell you how many students, as well as a small hand-full of college students who are pre-service teachers, verbalize death narratives. This journal entry written by an older teen, who is a college freshman, tragically illuminates the path of devastation and destruction felt by many of our young adults today.

Flights-of-the-mind plague those who are emotionally unhealthy by deadening their ability to grasp meaning and a purpose. There is way too great of a gap that exists to allow for an unfolding of a life's purpose. Who will be there to bridge this chasm between insanity and peace? Who/what is to be held responsible for this unpardonable human tragedy called emotional illness and the inescapable life traumas? Are the judge and jury of our society going to continue to cast boulders at the parents, the media, peer groups, or perhaps teachers? This young man, like countless others, are alive but walking dead. Their pain is inhumane. There is a large preponderance of students within our classrooms whose minds are in flight and whose landing strip is the morgue.

Perhaps those who are called to seal that societal crevices and thereby free the germination of seeds that grow purpose, are educators and parents. An intense examination of this young man's journal writing is frightening. It appears that the only *realness* that this young man senses is the entrapment of pitch-black water in the darkest of caves that holds his tormented mind in bondage. His candid words are inner thoughts that have violently erupted from an interminable volcano. His manifestation of *realness* is NOT one of unconditional love, rather, the continual molten lava of life that burns his spirit beyond recognition. His writing must be an invaluable memoir that must be placed at the forefront of everything we do as teachers and parents. As educators, what are we to do with narratives of this magnitude and what do they have to do with the meaning or lack of it in life?

Max Van Manen, author and educator in Canada and the Netherlands argues that everything must be understood in light of the unique nature of each human situation. We would also like to add the words "human frailty" into that equation. Everything in schools needs to be examined in light of each human situation and in the context of our human frailty! His text, *Researching Lived Experience,* voices his discontent with relying totally on abstract generalizations and theories (traditional approaches derived from using the behavioral or natural sciences). His writing supports our plea to educators and policymakers alike, to examine students in light of their lived experience. He states, "Pedagogy is the activity of teaching, parenting, educating, or generally living with children, that requires constant practical acting in concrete situations and relations."

Furthermore, he advocates that *where one stands* in their choice of research (quantitative versus qualitative—limited response/unyielding tests versus authentic assessments of human experiences) may be an indicator of both their pedagogical commitment and how one stands in life as an educator. One's research platform, in and of itself, is also an indicator of one's life purpose. His work clearly supports the claim that we must pedagogically-act out of a child's narratives and human experiences rather than from a superimposed set of predetermined mandates. The riveting journal entry (human experience) from our older teen requires us to ask ourselves this question, "What does a student's tremendous pain, devastation, and loss of life's meaning have to do with the way in which we teach and assess?" In other words, can these real-life painful experiences be used as a catalyst to inform purpose and pedagogy? Van Manen would say, "Absolutely yes"!

As we make our way in schools, educators continue to request criteria and/or red flags that will identify students who are in great pain. Are there any predictors of students who are at risk for having a deep connection with pain? After all, children as young as five years of age are beginning to speak a "suicide discourse". We do have what we believe is a formula for determining potential pain in students from as early as preschool and as late as completing one's life journey. Are you ready? The sure-fired formula for determining and/or predicting pain in students is called "ALL". Yep, that's correct—ALL!!

All students are in, or will be in pain during their life in schools. All students, regardless, will grow seeds of pain, hopelessness and/or rejection—three constants within a typical and atypical school/university. These three sobering words are the silent sledgehammers penetrating the self-efficacy of every student. Within the mind of a teacher, these three words outweigh any mandate, standard, benchmark and grade level expectation! Yet, these words and their seeds of devastation usually fall upon the barren emotional grounds called institutions of learning.

Why are we, as a nation, refusing to research and retool education in light of the human experience and frailty inherent within all of us? Who will listen? Who is going to act? Sadly, the voices and cries of our students and their families usually find little solace within the vicious bureaucratic constructs called a school or university.   After all, student success is still predominantly measured by rigid, standardized and/or teacher-made tests that are created void of the human experience. Allow us to say this resounding statement again. ***Mandates and assessments VOID of the human experience is an unethical act victimizing every child and teacher!*** Imagine if our accountability/assessment efforts were driven by how much we, as educators, reduced pain and freed students' minds to fully realize their potential—is this, perhaps, our most pressing moral mandate as educators? Why don't we ever ***get-it*** that affect supersedes cognition before learning can authentically take place?   Affective teaching equals cognitive learning. Qualitative informs quantitative. Both inform purpose.

A heart-rending, thought-stirring question might be, "What do pain, hopelessness, and rejection have to do with seizing one's meaning and purpose? To begin with, let us explore this question by first acknowledging some principles.

Pain, hopelessness, and rejection are cruel themes permeating one's literal life.   Human suffering is not a myth, fairytale or legend—it is our lived and living experiences. Disease, divorce, poverty, failure, addiction, suicide, and abuse are life's ruthless ruins of the human experience. When the human condition is catapulted into a tsunami of emotional or physical affliction, the fantasy of life comes to an abrupt halt! That once-captivating romance novel is tucked away to gather dust. We now say ... "Reality has set in!" But ...hold on ... there is HOPE. Teachers are musicians playing vibrant instruments of hope and joy."

We would like to further the notion that the reality of pain, if deconstructed properly, reaps a plentiful harvest called purpose. We have to understand that there are children in our classrooms who exist as silent-sufferers. To an onlooker, they may appear to be lazy, unmotivated, uninterested and even quiet. Could it be true that these **silent-sufferers** are simply struggling with an unquiet mind--one **they** cannot even understand? Do we really believe, wholeheartedly, that many of their intense behaviors are premeditated acts of disobedience wrought out of deviance? Are the uncompromising levels of "craziness" in our world really the judge and jury upon which we craft a destiny for our students? The diversity and increasing preponderance of mental and emotional illnesses that haunts our children are overwhelming. How do we, as educators, know the differences between an illness and deviancy? Furthermore, educators and parents have their own struggles in life that complicates and enflames the behavior of the child. Are we willing to acknowledge our own shortcomings rather than sit in the judge's chair and demand a verdict? An ancient master teacher once said, "He who is without sin, cast the first stone." Hmmm . . . gives us all something to think about. Let's now draw the parallel . . . If the 250 great minds of our era are not privy to capturing the untainted meaning of life, why not turn to the provoked minds, those who are continually victimized by the emotional deep ravines and high climbs of life. Let us use these inauspicious thinkers, those plagued with severe emotional disorders, to set the bar for discovering purpose and meaning and possibly rethink how we assess students. What can we learn from the precious brothers and sister of ours that deal daily with the bizarre, the frenetic, and the psychotic? Allow us to investigate how someone encapsulated with a severe emotional illness created productivity and purpose within her life.

Let us turn to a national bestseller by Kay R. Jamison entitled, **An Unquiet Mind**. During the time of publication, she was a Professor of Psychiatry at the John Hopkins University School of Medicine. As a recipient of numerous national and international scientific awards, she chronicles her own attacks of psychosis and how this illness afforded her dynamic meaning and artful purpose. She writes, "It has been difficult at times to weave together the scientific discipline of my intellectual field with the more compelling realities of my own emotional experiences. And yet it has been from this binding of raw emotion to the more distanced eye of clinical science that I feel I have obtained the freedom to live the kind of life I wanted and the human experiences necessary to try and make a difference in public awareness and clinical practice." We were thrilled that Dr. Jamison artfully verbalized the junction within raw emotion and career as the intersection where her purpose was crafted and meaning engendered. A writer from the ***Washington Post Book World*** states, "Jamison's strength is in the gutsy way she has made her disease her life's work and in her brilliant ability to convey its joys and its anguish . . . Extraordinary."

Dr. Jamison speaks about her experiences during her high school years. She cries, "I was deeply unhappy. . . I spent most of my time in tears or writing letters to my boyfriend . . . I was a senior in high school when I had my first attack. . . I lost my mind rather rapidly . . . nothing made sense . . . I could not begin to follow the material presented in my classes, and I would find myself staring out the window with no idea of what was going on around me . . . I have no idea how I managed to pass as normal in school, except that other people are generally caught up in their own lives and seldom notice despair in others if those despairing make an effort to disguise the pain . . . It was impossible to avoid quite terrible wounds to both my mind and heart—the knowledge that my thoughts had been so completely out of control, and the realization that I had been so depressed that I wanted only to die . . . I was amazed I survived, that I survived, that I survived on my own, and that high school contained such complicated life and palpable death . . . such a loss of one's self, with such proximity to death, and such distance from shelter." Colleagues, this is an example of the inhumane pain that goes virtually unnoticed within the halls and classrooms that many of our children, teachers, administrators, and parents grace.

Jamison, as well as an endless surplus of students sharing emotional holocausts, were/are entangled in a web of death. But what about their "Place of Further Still"? Can entry be plausible for those in emotional crises? What about their potential for realizing their purpose?

The early genius concealed within their "Place of Further Still" lies dormant, smothered under a harsh blanket of judgment and premature death. Their minds lay comatose upon a gurney where endless consumptions of death encase them. Who will rescue them? Who will have the courage to love them unconditionally? Who will be the 'Skin Horse' in their life that will discern the term 'real'? Allow us to again ask the question, "Where does one go when they have virtually lost all meaning and purpose?"

We unequivocally believe that we can ONLY find meaning and life's purpose in our human fragility. Fragility grows purposeful seeds and seeds of purpose. *We believe that there is no mandate more viable and more humane than one that is sold-out to improving the human condition.* This is our corporate purpose as educators and, very honestly, as human beings alike. How often we have said that the real lessons of life are bred during tumultuous times when we fall HARD and are pulled within a deep and dark, spiraling abyss. This abyss has the potential to be a profound wake-up call engaging one's contemplation-station! It is when we are in the depths of despair, realizing that we are easily broken, that our ears can finally hear and the blindfold from our eyes removed. We have now arrived at "The Place of Further Still" and are set-apart from the abyss while being majestically elevated to a higher ground. That higher ground is one's firm foundation of faith, hope and inner strength. *Failing is really falling forward; when we plummet, we are really in launch position.* BUT . . . will we take the challenge and launch ourselves where we need to be in order to move our life forward? Or, will we choose to remain stagnant and full of blame and victimization? *It is within the depths of endless pain, dark hopelessness, and riveting rejection that our purpose is unfolded and meaning illuminated.* Jamison closes out her book with fervent contemplation—contemplation marinated in action. She proclaims:

"We all build internal sea walls to keep at bay the sadness of life and the often overwhelming forces within our minds . . . One of the most difficult problems is to construct these barriers of such a height and strength that one has a true harbor, a sanctuary away from crippling turmoil and pain, but permeable enough, to let in fresh seawater that will fend off the inevitable inclination toward brackishness . . . But love is, to me, the ultimately more extraordinary part of the breakwater wall: it helps to shut out the terror and awfulness, while, at the same time, allowing in life and beauty and vitality . . . So why would I want anything to do with this illness? I honestly believe that as a result of it I have felt more things, more deeply; had more experiences, more intensely; loved more, and have been more loved . . ."

(Wow, Dr. Jamison . . . we are humbled by your figurative portrait; a humble portrayal articulating the intersection where your pain and joy met to craft your human call. Clearly, you have miraculously modeled how those with an unquiet mind have been given access to uncovering the real purpose and meaning for life . . . we applaud you!)

Pain, and all that encases it, has the potential to be the greatest explorer of human life. It births meaning and purpose. In light of education, a healing of the human condition, toward the unfolding of a student's individual life purpose, is our most pressing and moral mandate! Excruciating pain allows for an exploration of the most hidden questions of the heart. Through almost unbearable contemplation, exhaustingly, one is led into praxis that is inexplicably transparent within "The Place of Further Still". It is here where the

seedlings of meaning and purpose are miraculously sewn. An educator is the seamstress upon which the fabric of our nation is sewn.

    To close out this chapter, let us revisit the book, ***Tuck Everlasting***. The setting takes place in a rather "ho-hum" world where the human heart and mind are hungry for adventure. This is a fantasy novel that moves everyday life to a higher ground where the procession of majestic magnitude marches forth. ***Tuck Everlasting*** transforms the imagination to another dimension allowing them to aspire outside-of-self and frame their world in a different, more compelling way. ***Dreaming is a breathtaking mechanism that parades our imagination in front of our rational mind.*** Dreaming moves us into a realm that allows us to touch the hem of the Divine. Paul Fenimore Cooper, fantasy writer, advocates:

"He who lacks imagination
lives but one-half a life.
He has his experiences,
he has his facts,
he has his learning.
But do any of these really live
unless touched by the magic of imagination?"

    What decision did Winnie make regarding whether or not to drink from the spring of immortality? Well . . . she chose ***not*** to partake of the magic water but poured it instead upon a toad, leaving herself open to the final curtain call of nature. The ending portrays Jessie standing over her grave, silently reflecting upon the "what if's". ***Tuck Everlasting*** delivers death offstage, which is a subtle way of telling us about Winnie's fate, and at the same time, the Epilogue affirms that water was an instrument of youth for those who chose to partake. We wholly believe that Winnie's vast experiences at home and in the forest; her pain, frustration, fantasy and love, were catalysts in her finally coming to terms with her choice in favor of human frailty. Her life's purpose was beginning to emerge prior to her making the monumental decision to abstain. Thomas Edison reminds us that, "Restlessness and discontent are the first necessities of progress". Her purpose and meaning for her life crystallized and she made her decision to embrace the human condition. To a large degree, we believe that Jessie was envious of her choice, her mortality, her inner strength and a life's beautiful unfolding of purpose. After all, he now has no choice, no fate, and no eternal future beyond a physical coffin called earth. His longings and dreams were limited by a repetitive "lower ground". His fountain of youth had become a dried-up, holocaust of the mind. You see . . . Jessie's life will forever be calculated, prescribed and measured by a rigid set mandates and standards governing *human* immortality.

Close curtain . . .

Chapter 3
"Rekindling Purpose and Extinguishing the Flames of Negativity!"

It's wonderful to be in midlife; the hallmark point between young and old, folly and wisdom, children and grandchildren, paycheck and social security, pimples and lines, basket and casket in which we are moving from a twinkle to a wrinkle, from the womb to the tomb! Candidly, it is at that juncture that your "innards" go rather ballistic and you start cramming for the forthcoming final exam of life. Figuratively, you enter into a reflective circus funhouse full of mirror images of yourself from your days as a child until present. Each image has a vivid, sharp reflection that reminds one of their seasonal life changes. Those of us in our middle years can certainly attest to moving from the bleachers to the front section of life (always wanted to sit in the front row of something)! Hopefully, we have gathered life skills that meticulously intermingle a historian and visionary. Many will say that we have, "Come to age". Furthermore, the lines upon our face have been ingeniously drawn in order for one's life to be chronicled! If there were several contours upon your face and you had to have something written upon them that exemplified what you stand/stood for—what would your face illuminate? Interesting question, isn't it? Is it feasible that these words would visibly display our motives, beliefs, journey, as well as human fragility? Wouldn't these lines also attest to our human condition?

Think for just a moment. Wouldn't the phrases, words, or symbols reveal a sketch; a silhouette of emotions? We have seen many of life's portraits painted on the faces of our colleagues, parents, and students. The range of images is rather overwhelming to say the least. Sadly, on many occasions we evidence face narratives of a pathetic creature seemingly without will or purpose in life; one that is self-indulging, stricken with a gross absence of human dignity. As we earlier stated, some individuals possess life narratives that portray an obsession with the materialistic. They are full-of-self and try feverishly to live success (what ever that means) by the world's standards. But it is never too late to make a transition and journey into one's purpose. We must look at the truth of where we are, where we've been, and where we want to go—life's rather curious mathematical equation!

The ***un-shattered mirror of truth*** reflects life's essays written upon our faces. The sum total of all of the words and phrases would serve as a final epithet that showcases how we breathed meaning or deadly carbon monoxide into our life. How many people do you know who STAND for something other than on a pedestal that positions themselves as statues of liberty? Many maneuver life ***just existing***; their visage is vaporous, not victorious. Their heart calloused, continually scabbed over from life's repetitive, self-inflicting wounds, promoting the old ***poor me*** and ***playing the victim*** 24-7! These individuals act much like the fictitious character Eeyore, the old, grey donkey who co-stars with Winnie-the-Pooh and Tigger. A.A. Milne created Eeyore's pessimistic disposition to offset Pooh Bear who is full of fluff and adores life and all that it holds. And then there is their sidekick Tigger . . . who continually sings, "I'm bouncy, bouncy, bouncy, bouncy . . . fun, fun, fun, fun, fun!" What a gleesome-threesome whose characteristics are easily differentiated and diverse dispositions contagiously illuminated! Their temperaments inform and create their character. Colleagues, are you an Eeyore, Pooh Bear, or Tigger? How would others peg you?

Do our facial lifelines reveal character or a caricature? This question will serve as the impetus for our next chapter in which we examine the dispositions of those "called" into the realm of teaching. Our last two chapters are the foundation upon which to build a precipice that will vigorously respond to our hunger for purpose and purposeful teaching. Many books about teaching will dance around the notion of purpose or they will completely abstain from speaking about it. After all, the very essence of the word ***purpose*** congers up images with spiritual and religious overtones.

Why do we shy away from the spiritual as educators? Answer--because we feel that it is offensive and off limits. Many of us have been taught that spiritual is territorial and belongs only at home or place of worship. Our question is, "Does McDonald's restaurant shy away from hamburgers?" Absolutely not! Why? Because hamburgers are at the forefront of their success and marketing—it's their foundation and building! As educators, purpose is our foundation and building and it exists in a realm well beyond what our finite minds can dictate and define! Purposeful teaching, teaching that is under the headship of a saintly call (teaching at the intersection where content meets the fragile human condition) is the spiritual essence of our work.

Parker J. Palmer, master teacher and author, has written a text entitled, ***To Know As We Are Known: Education as a Spiritual Journey.*** He states, "My vocation (to use the poet's term) is the spiritual life, the quest for God, which relies on the eye of the heart. My avocation is education, the quest for knowledge, which relies on the eye of the mind. I have seen life through both these eyes as long as I can remember—but the two images have not always coincided . . . In this secular age, with religion on the wrong side of the fact-fantasy divide, it may seem odd to turn to spirituality for a new way of knowing. I do so because I am ultimately concerned not only with knowledge but with truth." Palmer's books and many keynote addresses acknowledge the pain that he also sees permeating education, in particular, with teachers. He refers to this as "the pain of disconnection". He states, "Everywhere I go, I meet faculty who feel disconnected from their colleagues, from their students, and from their own hearts." With great enthusiasm, we come along side our colleague in his attempt to authenticate education and unfold how exciting and joyful teaching will become when driven by a spiritual summons.

As we stated earlier, midlife and the reflections that grow out of it, causes one to stop, reflect, and rethink what is crucial. Midlife breeds a reshuffling of priorities. Clearly, our many years as educators and parents have allowed us to synthesize experiences, priorities, and observations that we evidence in schools. We have and continue to see a malaise in the demeanor of educators as well as within the parent constituency. For teachers, much of the destruction in our attitudes is due to the paradox that we mentioned in the last chapter, e.g., the students that are severely-challenged and still judged on the merit of how they can jump through the hoops of many developmentally inappropriate assessments and standards. Other obstacles aiding in the malaise of teacher attitudes are irrational accountability demands, rigid curriculum, unrealistic expectations, unyielding one-size-fits-all pre-packaged instruction, and some mandates that go against every fiber of our being. For parents, we all are still trying to figure it out and rarely feel equipped and able to raise our children in an ever-changing, increasing unprincipled world! For both teacher and parent, much of the malaise has to do with the relentless complexities and challenges of everyday life. After all . . . LIFE HAPPENS!

Where do exhausted teachers go who try to keep their calling alive? Many of these teachers have retreated to their own classrooms. They find solace-in-self. It's rather easy to fall victim to copping an "Eeyore attitude" when you battle against forces that measure the integrity of a teacher and student void of the human experience. Teachers are in the trenches fighting desperately for kids while some of the generals destroy the very ammunition that allows them to teach and reach students. After all, a soldier will surely die on the battlefield when all sides are coming at him, including his own platoon! What happens when one is all caught up in a whirlwind of attacks? The answer is that they go into a ***protection-mode*** and seek withdrawal. We can't tell you how often we witness teacher disenchantment. This protection-mode inhibits the unfolding or furthering of one's life purpose. It also stifles and stuns one's calling. A disgruntled heart may eventually turn into a selfish disposition. In fact, we believe that selfishness has swallowed humanity. Those swallowed will lose sight of their purpose and will try repeatedly to find it in the wrong places and with a wrong motivation.

We continue to interview many students and have asked them to tell us what bugs them most about adults. Overwhelmingly, they see adults, including teachers, manifesting relentless duplicity on a daily basis. Imagine being a secondary student and changing classes while witnessing hypocritical discourse in 1st hour, 2nd hour, 3rd hour, etc. Our students are telling us that an educator's walk doesn't recognize their talk. We, as educators, can certainly talk it (we can lecture like no other species alive), but seem to struggle greatly today with consistency within our walk! Some educators stand in front of their students with megaphones and act as drill sergeants commanding respect and caring. They are quick to hand out detentions for disrespect and demeaning behaviors, yet their own discourse parallels and sets the bar for their students. The fruit will eventually not fall far from the fruitcake! Their students will eventually manifest their same behaviors! That old ***do what I say, not as I do*** stuff doesn't cut it! We have to stop the dichotomy!

We continually hear stories of teachers making their way to the teachers' lounge only to verbally filet colleagues and elicit zero compassion or caring. We continue to hear war stories and testimonies from teachers about the horrors of their colleagues who won't even speak to them in the halls, much less acknowledge when they are hurting. Our telephone rings weekly from principals who plead with us for help in connecting a vastly divided faculty. Principals stand in bewilderment as to how such great individuals, outside of the school, are caught up within their building, participating in cheap, petty backbiting and gossip. These are the principals that carry a rich, vibrant vision for their staff and students and continue to knock their heads against the walls daily for answers. These are not the administrators who have fallen victim to the same negativity. Colleagues', witnessing a divided faculty is now the rule rather than the exception in most of the schools that we serve and study. Of course, there are varying levels of this in all settings. A school and staff divided against itself will eventually fall and crumble.

When we are called to work with a struggling staff, our first intervention is ***extreme*** team-building with a large dosage of compassion training. During the many team-building exercises we see the cancerous growths that are debilitating and destroying their power and potential as a team of professionals. The seeds of purpose cannot grow when the ground is filled with thorns and weeds! On many occasions we witness very small pockets of faculty who are manifesting racism, sexism, ageism, and length-of-time-teaching-ism toward their comrades, parents, and students. These colleagues have fallen *way* off the slippery slope and need a life makeover and an exiting of their classroom. Their demeanors are the destroyers of children and families. Within our world and individual communities, it seems that everybody is mad at everybody, doesn't it? SO MUCH ANGER! Many cannot even account for a reason, yet, they are constantly argumentative, upset, and pride themselves on being/becoming drama queens/kings! They enjoy the power and attention that their anger breeds. Many of those who take on that disposition are also sold-out to revenge and restitution. Not only do we evidence road rage, we witness classroom rage, staff meeting rage, homecoming rage, recess rage, parent rage; all of which are gaining speed! *As anger builds, purpose is destroyed and our calling will transform into a brawling.* If we are going to rekindle or discover our purpose, we need to, as Patti LaBelle reminds us in a song . . . take on "A NEW ATTITUDE".

Many educators are fervent about adopting such incredible programs such as "Character Counts" or other quality affective training programs. *Instructor Magazine* in 1999 dedicated an entire edition to "Character Education". Within that edition, editor Carol Mauro-Noon states, "By aiming for the highest common denominator among humankind—something much of the television news and certain print media might well consider—character-education programs are promoting positive behavioral change." They report that character is making a comeback and the learning of "old-fashion values, once a homegrown, natural skill formally seems to have fallen out of vogue in recent years". Should teachers also exemplify good character? Richard Osguthorpe, Brigham Young University, posed this query in his dissertation, a part of which he presented at the McKay School of

Education as he addressed the theme, ***"The relationship between the moral character of a teacher and the moral development of a student."*** Osguthorpe gathered his data from "The Manner in Teaching Project" a 3-year study in two schools involving 11 teachers and their students, grades K-8. The study questioned how a teacher's virtuous traits would be displayed in his/her conduct and how they would influence students. It seems impossible to define ***how*** virtuous a teacher must be to have a positive and everlasting influence upon their students. His research attests to the fact that teachers, as role models, possess great influence and power. A teacher's character is one that is watched closely and often mimicked by those who follow in their footsteps.

Our desire in sharing our experiences regarding the negativity that we see is not to tattle tale or to brutally attack our calling. NO WAY, NO HOW! Many of our readers may feel that we have spent way to much time dwelling upon the negative. Yet, a cancerous growth must be exposed and removed before full healing and rekindling of purpose can take place. The driving force behind our forthrightness is to place an imprint upon our minds and fire within our hearts to always be heads-up about our demeanor, in particular, our words and body language.

The figurative language gestured by our body can serve as a thermometer for one's motives and disposition. The emotional temperature of a school and classroom can be easily assessed by the heat or coldness that the bodies inside it emit. There are many, many teachers and administrators that we witness that are extraordinary, empowering, and never strike with an unkind chord. They have told us that they make a decision everyday to be joyful and life-giving. Colleagues, here is a challenge for us all . . Upon entering any institution of learning, can we vow to be totally abstinent from words, actions, and interactions that rip apart the strong fabric of our

nation—that is, our fellow teachers, our students and their families? Remember, TEACHING IS A CALLING NOT A BRAWLING!

As educators, children look to us as a mirror upon which to reflect a dynamic life. We are mirrors of reflection and refraction! We are still considered by some to be powerful role models. Do we realize that parents also look to us for a model to roll/role after! Many of our parents are really disgruntled children in older bodies. How frightening! Do we really think our students and parents are oblivious to the selfish motives we may elicit? We can learn ***boocoodles*** from the young children and even young parents (as we witnessed in an earlier chapter) who have not yet been completely tarnished and tattered by our world. Kindergarteners and younger children do not care how many degrees we hold, what kind of designer clothes we wear, if we are a member of the union, or what our ethnic texture is. They just want someone to love them and believe in them. ***They want a teacher sold-out to purpose.*** They can spot a fake a mile away. They also have photographic memories. They remember more about what they see rather than what they hear. Bummer!

We believe that if fervent soul-searching took place and finding and claiming purpose was at the forefront of our work as teachers; outrageous joy would be restored and our vaporous lives would be drastically changed. Remember, we must leave the comfort of complacency, especially in times of great upheaval, in order to know where we came from! It is a journey of restoration and renewal . . .a captivating adventure in the human condition.

Shortly, we will introduce to you a vibrant pathway for discovering and carving out a purpose; one that seeks to renew and restore joy within your soul. If you continue your journey with us, you will secure many needed tools to reawaken that which has seemingly been obliterated or set aside. Upon completion of your laborious task in discovering purpose, you will discover that ***no one will recognize the new you***! Others will think that you have had a life-makeover! They will be convinced that you are America's NEXT HOT ROLE MODEL! The chalkboard in your classroom will also jump-for-joy along with those who study under your tutelage. Imagine a chalkboard that is now filled with anticipation and stands in awe of every word that you will place upon it! Our upcoming instruction may help take you on an alternative pathway toward rethinking and reconceptualizing the question, "What is the meaning of life?" It is rather simple, but will require deep reflection on your part. Anytime we want to move forward in life, we must first execute some deep, honest self-reflection, called contemplation. Following contemplation, action must be taken (remember contemplation and action moonlight as identical twins)! Ready . . . 9 - 10 – 11 - 12

Many times, contemplation will expose problems and issues that deem resolving. ***Identification of the problem*** is clearly the first step. While many people can clearly articulate the dilemma, they refuse to get off their patty-melts and take the next step. Many are too lazy and relish in their misery. Misery loves company and disgruntled company loves misery as its ***only*** source entertainment. After all, it's definitely easier for us to blame and remain. How often do adults admit that they have major struggles yet are caught up in the "blame game" and cannot and do not desire to move forward. Some get caught up and excited about analyzing the problem yet become a pillar-of-salt when asked to take the next step. Remember, too much analysis causes paralysis! ***Taking ownership and full accountability in fixing what is broken*** is a very challenging next step. It's not for the weak-minded. Realistically, many are still in great pain and cannot even fathom a mustard seedling of hope. Some desire to move, yet are thoroughly emotionally drained and stuck. Our hearts go out to them. We acknowledge their pain and continue to support them in receiving intervention to assist them in taking that next gigantic step.

Moving ahead and piloting our problems/issues means that we take flight and soar above them rather than sitting unmoved, hidden within life's brutal baggage compartment. Taking-off of life's jagged runway means that we boldly respond to these flight simulator questions. Am I actually ready to take flight or am I continually grounded by life's severe weather pattern? After all, a fledging bird must eventually abort the nest and test its soaring capacity even during turbulent storms. WHAT WILL I ACTUALLY BE DOING TO CREATE THE CHANGE IN THE FORECAST? How will my flight plan be different? Remember that change is a process not an event. It is the process that grows-us-up to embrace the prize which is an effervescent strengthening of ourselves toward JOYFULLY uplifting and catapulting others into flight. Again, it is the flight of contemplation and action.

There is a multitude of books that focus upon discovering meaning within our life. Clearly, one can easily measure the tenor of society by the content and shear number of self-help materials. It appears that our 21st century is inundated with fix-its! Everyone has a fix-it system for every ill that penetrates society. Admittedly, many of them are very helpful in taking needed action. Yet, the problem is that many of us are immune from the cheap, pop cultural antibiotics that are marketed as quick-fixes to a life-long problem! We have had it up to our eyebrows with instant recipes and pseudo-steps for success (whatever that means). Many people journey from program to program, believing that around the corner their eyes will be miraculously opened, problem resolved, and their joy rejuvenated. Sadly, some (hear us . . . SOME) self-help engenders self-helplessness or a blaming-of-the-other syndrome.

Some self-help stuff is a mechanism to engender poor-me or self-victimization! On the other hand, many self-help avenues give people the JOLT they need to take the next steps. We applaud those life-giving entities! Bravo!

Why are we trying to drive home the insistence of purpose when there are so many other very critical aspects within teaching that need emphasis? We absolutely believe finding meaning and rekindling purpose IS a critical issue facing all educators. Admittedly, many educators tell us they have lost their vision for students and have never crafted or tweaked a purpose that they can claim for themselves. They have lost sight as to the original reason why they said *yes* to children and families. They truly cannot articulate a purpose and meaning for their life. If you don't believe us . . . we challenge you to ask any individual on the street to describe their purpose and meaning for life. We have actually done this with many people, young and older, across various geographical areas, social economic means, gender, and ethnicity. As a whole, people tell us that their purpose is their children, their job, to have enough money to retire, the caretaking of a loved one, or even just surviving. Many older adults and those in poorer areas speak of their ability to *just survive* and we are humbled by their tenacity to care for themselves and those they love. On rare occasions and in more affluent areas, some truthfully declare to us that their purpose is themselves. Worldly success has many of them by the tail! Wow—how incredibly sad.

Interestingly enough, many of our hearts are big and our troubles even bigger. Finding purpose IS IN NO WAY correlated to less problems and troubles within a lifetime. In fact, when one discovers their meaning, they become driven to improve the human condition WHICH entertains more issues. They fervently seek-out problems and folks-in-crisis! In other words, finding or rekindling purpose means we open ourselves up to serve others (not self) with great diligence and persistence. ***When one serves another, one's self is vigorously served.*** Purpose does not engender boredom or complacency—it defines joy!

PurposeLESS people cannot breathe life-changing breath, their empty words are just that—vaporous! They verbalize their commitment to our youth and do strive to make a difference, but are caught within the confines of the self. PurposeFULL people transform and restore lives. They celebrate the otherness of life. How does one go about discovering and carving out an individual, uniquely crafted purpose? As purpose-driven teachers, we are called much like superheroes; to hold fast and embrace the highest decent and ethical standards for living—to sell it all and serve! Living a stellar, purposeful life means modeling fervent charity, service, honesty, and acute compassion. Purpose knows no boundaries or compromise. As teachers, we first have to begin by re-setting the bar; raising the standard for teachers far above those we serve and over time, expect them to emulate our model.

To begin with, if you are one who adamantly believes that you have been called to teach, the following statement should make total sense to you. Ready? IT'S NOT ABOUT YOU! Say what? Let us state this again in another way. Revolutionizing lives and fulfilling our purpose means that it *ain't* about us. When teaching and purpose are reduced to serving one's self, our calling is melted down to create a self-charm bracelet. With great boldness and confidence we proclaim that the first step in uncovering and embracing purpose must start out with Unpopular Premise #1, "It's NOT About Us!" Our purpose within our life transcends what the world would sell us as a worthy bill of goods. The meaning of life is bred out of a purpose that far exceeds our individual personal fulfillment, needs, goals, happiness, and conception of peace. It extends beyond our friends, our family, and our work. It is far greater than any wild dream or exciting mission that we have envisioned! These thoughts certainly go against what many motivational speakers and consultants would promote. We did a brief Internet search and typed in several words to see what kind of propaganda is out there flirting with our purpose. Here are some of the titles that we retrieved that promised to be an answer to our problems:

> ***Be All You Can Be . . . Invest in Yourself . . . The Only Motivation is Self- Motivation . . . Setting and Attaining Your Goals . . . Ignite Yourself, The Ultimate Power Source . . . To Be An Effective Leader, Do a Check Up from the Neck Up. . . You Are Your Fortune . . . Get Rich Quick Baby . . . Market Yourself . . . Believe in Yourself or at Least Try To . . . You Can Make Millions . . . You Can Have It All, What is it You Want? . . . Can't See Yourself, Have Your VISION Checked . . . Peaking In on Your Personal Peak Performance. . . (And our favorite is the following) I'm Not Depressed; I'm Just Having a Lousy Conversation With Myself!***

We encourage you to try the same Internet search, it is quite a hoot! Please do not misunderstand; we are not poking fun at these websites, rather emphasizing how our pop culture propaganda commandeers our calling. Words such as personal, motivation, self, power, and money that are entered into a search engine will yield a focus on self. For each word that you enter, you will receive endless hits from companies, several of whom may be preying on our selfishness and hunger for self-actualization all in the name of what our world defines as successful (whatever that means!). We do recognize that there are many fine, respectable companies and private consultants that are integral in helping further the human condition.

Searching for purpose has a long history and has bamboozled people for hundreds of years. Why? We think we have a possible answer to that question, one that will NOT gain us entry into "America's Most Cherished Beliefs"! This brings us to another idea called Unpopular Premise #2 which is, "Complete Self-Focus is Hocus-Focus!" From an early age, life begins to bombard us with questions such as, "What should I be when I grow up . . . What kind of future will I have . . . Who will I fall in love with . . . Will I be successful (whatever that means!)? How can I have it all?"

An exhaustive, recurring focus on self is a "hocus focus" and always casts one on center-stage and at the starting and ending gate of life. Total self-immersion will never, ever, and in no way, unfold our purpose. A "Looking in the Mirror Approach" day after day without fervent reflection/contemplation causes us to obsess with success (whatever that means!). And, since all mirrors reflect differently, our image of ourselves will certainly vary drastically. Every day we could say, "Mirror, mirror on the wall . . . today what purpose shall I call"? Discovering a life purpose transforms our journey from *self-centered* to *other-centered.* It moves us from self-satisfaction to steward-compassion.

We believe that educators, by our very name, thrive to aspire and journey outside of ourselves and to arrive fully into others. We, as teachers, have come to serve, not be served. Certainly we do not want to become fresh prey for our world's predator called "success" (whatever that means!) The intoxicating reality is that we could exceed every self-goal, overachieve every dream, and be endowed with all of that our world deems as being successful (whatever that means!) and still lose sight of life's meaning. Yes, we can embellish it all and still miss the most rewarding nuggets inherent in uncovering one's life purpose.

Now, let's open up the flood gates that will lead to discerning your life's purpose. First, we will present a quick lesson in the power of the historical with regard to words. As you know, the study of words is called etymology. The origin and usage of words can be one of the most dynamic studies for both a teacher and student. We will use both mortar and brick to build a foundation upon which to build the term purpose. To begin with, the word "purpose" is conceived out of several Greek words whose different spelling indicates different contextual usages. Studying its early usage lures us into the richness of the language and how it is presented within the shades of the meaning regarding some common idea. Within the Greek language, there can be upward to fifty or more words, including the compounds that may be used to express one general thought. The employment of each one of these words has precise historical and contextual significance. The rule is usually twofold. First, there are many different Greek words that could complement one English word. Second, there is vastly contextualized English meanings attached to one single word.

Retrieving the original and ancient meanings of words dynamically form the foundation upon which to begin the study of purpose. Excavating its historical meanings using lexicons, speaks volumes if we will really hear, not just listen. The Ancient Greek terms engenders definitions rich in substance that envisions horizons upon which we, as teachers, can receive our calling. The following are English translations for the word "purpose" that has been translated from Ancient Greek. Remember that words are not static things. Terms and their meanings change drastically over time—they are evolutionary! Again, these forthcoming English meanings are translations derived from the Greek Language.

The Original and Ancient meanings of the term "Purpose" is:

- A Decree
- A Foreshadowing
- Quality of Being Determined
- Reason for Being
- A Deliberate Intention
- To Come to Be
- Terminally Resolve
- To Consult or Take Counsel

- A Sense of Predestinate Inevitability
- To Bring Forth or Forward
- Reason for Being

We absolutely believe that the original conception of purpose was/is a forthright declaration of independence and resounding proclamation of one's emanate calling. A calling is an affirmation and living tribute; a testimony and manifestation of one's purpose. A call infers an inner urge or spiritual prompting. *A call* is a setting-apart from the rest. In other words, those called to teach are those who have been called-out and set-apart from the whole for a specific duty. Our true meaning in/of life comes only when we humbly take refuge within "The Place of Further Still". It is within this domain that we carve out our unique life purpose and willingly respond to the forthcoming call to serve. When we cross into the threshold of "The Place of Further Still" we claim the heart's *pre-ordained right of passage* to beckon three entities that will give testimony as to our life purpose. These three entities, which we will call the "3 P's", are the foremost predictors of purpose. Now, if you will please, sit down, get out a piece of paper, and jot down three letter 'P's' somewhere on your page. O.K., here we go!

The first "P" stands for the entity called 'PAIN'. We would like for you to make one of the 'P' words into the word PAIN and draw a line under it. First, list all of the different types of pain that you have felt or are feeling within your life up to this point. For example, if you were abused as a child, write that down; or had/ have an eating disorder, make that notation; or you might have had a parent that struggled with alcoholism; jot all of those very painful realities down. Nothing is insignificant and every word, notation, and feeling is vitally relevant. Pain is an integral part of painting our portrait of purpose. *The harsh, colored splashes of pain on a life's canvas are the brushes that display a gloomy, lifeless, and seemingly endless silhouette of agony.* Pain, and all of the desperation, fear, and suffering that it engenders, is critical to recall and record. Allow us to give you an example from one of our own lives:

PAIN
- My Adoption
- Feelings of Abandonment
- Rejection
- Non-Acceptance/Unwanted
- Who Am I and Where Did I Come From?
- Teasing
- Where Do I Fit In?
- Feeling Unloved
- Nightmares
- Fear of Dying and Being Homeless
- Being Called 'Retarded'

Once you have made your list, the second step is to see if you can see any themes or relationships among your data. Look at the list above that depicts the most critical pain within one of our early lives (This is Elizabeth's list). What themes can you see? What painful portrait are these data painting? This brings us to the third step which is synthesis of the data. What are the dominant patterns that you see? What inferences can be drawn? In this case, there is an abundant amount of data that supports an obsession with feeling rejection.

Next . . . create a thesis (Say what?? You've gotta be kidding me! Hey chill out duuuude. . . after all; we make our students do this dreaded task, don't we?) We know that we are preaching to the preacher when we declare that writing a thesis statement is a dynamic tool to construct meaning. (Sounds like something a teacher might say!) In this instance, it helps us to witness the path of devastation and projectiles from the mind's spiraling tornado.

A critical examination of these data would certainly yield a thesis something like this, "Adoption and her early feelings of abandonment have manifest into fears and anxieties such as non-acceptance and homelessness". How about that for a thesis? Time to thank a teacher! The next task is one that is so important and necessary. What target populations (groups of students) would be best served given her experience with this type of pain? In other words, if non-acceptance and homelessness are the synthesized themes, what groups of people can Elizabeth reach given her pain in these areas? The populations may include adopted kids, drop outs, students with emotional challenges, adult and alternative education students, teen runaways, etc. Remember pain, and the torrents of nutrients that fertilize it, is an amazing and authorized predictor of purpose.

Looking into the past, and the baggage that we carry EVEN when we were not on vacation, helps one to assess progress and seek further healing. Remember that old verbiage, "hind-sight is 20/20"? Don't we all wish perfect foresight produced infallible insight? Interestingly enough, many who physically have no/ little eye sight, are those with perfect vision. Contemplation is the informant that tattle-tales on action—it holds our actions accountable! Remember, contemplation is generated through a surplus of action and action increases a manifold of contemplation. Contemplation may reveal a necessity for intervention. Again, many are able to diagnose a problem and many reflect upon the factors that were correlated to it. Yet, seeking the road that should be the most traveled is called the "Doing Expressway". Exploring painful residue will certainly reopen the wound. Yet, the infection that lays dormant festers and will eventfully need to be lanced. Bottom line; just be sure you are honest with yourself. Our vulnerability can be our worst sojourner for truth. We know that many of our healthiest people are those humbling themselves enough to seek intervention. They have come to a full knowledge that many of life's most abstract puzzles needs a professional to help piece it together.

Finally, can you articulate how pain has been an instrument for hope, renewal, and healing? This is so necessary. May your spirit be renewed as you find peace and forgiveness in your path of pain deconstruction. After our heart declares forgiveness, we are finally privy to boldly unleashing our potential and thereby helping others cope and hope. As we endure pain and suffering, our character is strengthened. We are miraculously form-fitted to clothe others who are left naked with pain. We call this concept "developmental-suffering", which is related to their first cousin called "developmentally-appropriate"! Ha. Get ready, this next statement is very profound (?). Ready . . . developmental means developmental! It rests on the principle that *when its time, its time* and you can't speed up a clock that's not plugged in! Developmental suffering (suffering over long periods of time that are famine-infested and emotionally-brutal) presents unbelievable opportunities to track our purpose IF we use it to help others envision horizons of hope. If life is one of our greatest of teachers, then surely we are destined to fall short of a perfect score. Last we heard, the race is far from perfect. Imagine having the pressure of executing perfection. Life's re-testing and re-teaching will increase our likelihood of acing the final, cumulative exam. If we never fall, how can we ever learn how to pick ourselves up? Remember, experience is our greatest teacher because it gives the tests first and lessons learned after. Each failed life-exam develops a stronger internal suffering mechanism that eventually opens the flood gates and one's purpose is left to run free!

As you continue to paint your portrait of pain, you can vividly see how each individual stroke of life's brush impacted your life. You probably also visualize how there are/were key individuals--Jiminy Crickets--that lightened your load and directed your wavering pathways. (Remember Jiminy Cricket? He was Pinocchio's conscience who showed up as a cricket dressed in a tuxedo and carrying an umbrella? His famous statement was, "Let your conscience be your guide!") These conscience-dwellers are those that provide us with rest, renewal, and ethics. How many of these *human rest areas upon life's highways* were teachers? Parker Palmer reminds us that, "If identity and integrity are found at the intersection of the forces that converge in our lives, revisiting some of the convergences that called us toward teaching may allow us to reclaim the selfhood from which good teaching comes". If you stare at your painful portrait, can you predict what people and groups might fall within your sphere of influence?   Please make note of these people or possibly groups of individuals (support groups, etc) that were a personal lean-to.

Now let's look at the second 'P' found upon your page. The second entity that needs to be unearthed from "The Place of Further Still" is that of "POWERSOURCE". The term *power* has an intriguing rooting, also. Once again, there are many Ancient Greek words for this one English term. Power denotes mighty works, right to act, freedom of action, strength, force, unrestricted, and signifies vigor. Consider the people that give you strength, vitality, energy, hope, replenishment, and extreme honesty? Theses individuals are our lighthouses and do not worry about how fast we grow, but how strong we grow! Before beginning the next exercise, we would like for you to consider several scenarios.

How many of you have viewed the movie, "The Perfect Storm"? This movie depicts fisherman who are not only zealous, but obsessive in finding a plethora of fish in order to gleam success (whatever that means!). As the story goes, they set out and eventually secure a location abundant with fish. While immersed on a fishing frenzy, an enormous storm appears on the horizon. A decision must be made quickly. The captain seeks out his ship-to-shore radio (his waterway powersource for potential problems) for a weather update. Upon hearing the news of a devastating storm approaching, the captain is confronted with a scruples question. Do he and his crew stay and make a haul with the hopes of negotiating the evil tempest and reaping their fortunes OR do they dump the fish and leave an angler's goldmine? Well . . . in a fury, they hurriedly fished and fished and fished and fished—the gallows were filled to the gills (pun intended)! The storm came, as predicted, and an outraged tsunami swallowed the crew and all perished (except for many of the fish—how ironic?) You see, they entered into the deepest of waters with the highest predictability of disaster, given the forecast. The captain disregarded the warning message (which was his lighthouse) that was blaring from his ship-to-shore transmitter. Forsaking his powersource, he sealed his destiny.

The moral of the story is:

"Enduring pain and emotional distress without powersources generates even greater pain and eventual peril".

Whom do you go to in times of great pain and frustration? Whom do you seek out for guidance? Do you have a mentor who has placed you under their sturdy wing? Do you have a strong faith and/or set of high ethical and moral standards that help frame your disposition? Who/what is your source of truth? In other words, "Who Ya Gonna Call?" (and the answer is not Ghostbusters!) We, as human beings, regardless of how breathtaking we are, need at least one person (usually the same gender) that will offer us *extreme* honesty. They boldly, yet in unconditional love, speak the truth. These are the individuals whose only motive is an unselfish motive! Their motto is, *seek to understand, rather than being understood.* They clearly understand our human frailties and are not judgmental, but instrumental. Their lighthouse is much like a Bed and Breakfast resort with all the amenities! Some will say, "I am my own lighthouse"! O.K. and your point is? What happens when the bulb goes out or you lose electricity? We do acknowledge that we have, within us, the potential to be very resourceful and have amazing abilities, but when the going-gets-tough, the tough may not be tough enough! We absolutely believe that there are many times when we must seek strength outside of ourselves and connect to the other. Our world continues to sell us counterfeit goods that guarantee that we can *always* do it ourselves.

The following are Elizabeth's identified lighthouses. Note the commonalities in the individuals that she selected.

POWERSOURCES

- Personal Faith
- Husband
- Wise, older (elderly) female mentors
- Women's study group
- Mother Theresa (role model for stewardship)
- Close female younger friend

Elizabeth's ***rest areas upon her doing-expressways*** were her faith, husband, and close female friends as well as identified stellar female role models. Each afforded her vigorous direction, transparent vision, and an endless fountain of wise counsel (some of which tasted very bitter). The truth can hurt! OUCH! After all, truth-in-love can be a very tortuous medication to swallow! Note: **You did not see the word "SELF" as a powersource that was listed.** Why? Is it because Elizabeth felt like she was a weak woman and incapable of solving her own problems? Not on your life!! In fact, the mightiest of women and men have powersources surging them forward daily. We ***are*** a source of strength for ourself and must use that energy alongside wise counsel. Yet, we absolutely believe that when someone is facing a personal holocaust of the mind (severe emotional trauma) they are vulnerable to falling victim to extreme fatigue and a potential physiological disease. These individuals usually cannot muster-up even a minimal rush of energy; rather they experience a total body-mind-soul power outage! Therefore, they need instruments of energy surges (powersources) to charge and recharge their being. Powersources are "Energizing Bunnies" in that they keep going . . . and going . . . and going! Love those television commercials!

Under the word ***Powersources***, begin to jot down individuals that have functioned as life-givers rather than life-takers. This would include any group of folks that have offered replenishment. Next, do you have any role models whose stellar life, ideas, and character is worthy of emulation? These ***highly***

principled character-walkers can be living or deceased, young and old, male and female, real or fictitious. List all of them. Next, record any attributes/dispositions they possess and that you were/are drawn to. Many times, what draws us to others is usually that which we desire and lack within ourselves. For example, if you attend a recovery group, you would highlight this particular group as a ***powersource*** with an attribute called "support". You may also want to ponder on how each individual/group handled crisis situations? Did they flee from trouble or confront it responsibly? This is a captivating and most critical question. There is much wisdom in examining how our mentors battle life's challenges. If you study the historical battle clothing (armor) of a soldier you will see that there is a thick metal covering protecting *just* the frontage of one in battle. Why? Is it because life's mercenaries are NOT to flee from combat, but confront it with great exuberance? Interesting possibility! Lastly, you may also want to record anything that has made an imprint upon your life and livelihood such as their quotes and/or precious sayings that identify them. Every thought is fair game. Many of us have grandmothers and grandfathers that have made profound statements that will forever be imprinted upon our hearts.

Powersources are just that—pillars of force! We strongly suggest that as you mature (a frightening thought); you also seek out much older, highly seasoned and salted adults whose penetrating knowledge is priceless. They see and perceive with such prophetic wisdom; in other words, they don't mince words! They TELL IT LIKE THEY SEE IT! Their motto is rather simple; don't B.S. just confess! They may appear physically slow, but DO NOT BE DECEIVED, they are not slothful. Remember, just because there is snow on their roof doesn't mean there ain't fire in the furnace! Lame! We need to handle them with care, love them up, and listen intently to their discourse of wisdom. Allow us to take a brief moment to share with you a true story that has the potential to close Hershey's down because it's so sweet!

One day we received a telephone call from an older man who was the adult leader in his men's group at his church. He asked if we would speak for about an hour to 25 of his friends. We immediately said, "Absolutely, Sir". We then asked him to give us a little more information including a little bit about his group and what content they would like us to speak about. He laughed and said, "Hey, we are just a bunch of old codgers, we'll like anything you beautiful girls have to say to us!" Shockingly, they were a special group of older men, whose ages ranged from 80 years old and older with many well into their nineties! Several had been doctors, lawyers, automobile workers, teachers, a basketball coach, a caterer who was now blind, and several gentle men from as assisted living center. How about that for a tough audience? We looked at each other and thought, "What could we have to say that would be of any significance to these precious grandfathers, great-grandfathers and great-great grandfathers?" We were excited about the opportunity to spend time with a strong, vibrant circle of such distinguished older men whose remarkable lives were leading them to the hundredth mark. We remarked to each other that we wanted to just show up, shut up, and listen to them rather than ourselves!

We began our presentation by putting our precious men in groups (after all we are teachers!). We had copied and enlarged a picture of a gigantic, treacherous mountain. We told them that they had been summoned by the Almighty to climb to the top of this mountain by themselves without any help or gear. They would be given no water, food, map, or light. We asked them to decide how and if, at their current age, they would make the journey. They were then to discuss this in their groups and be ready to report back to the entire group. We announced that they would have ten minutes to complete the task. Colleagues, you would have had your socks blessed off observing these ageless icons collaborate, draw routes, and outline specific steps. The end result is that they unanimously agreed that if they were called to do this, regardless of their age, they would ***unequivocally*** invest in the climb.

We asked each group to give us a report. Believe it or not, all 25 men had something to say! And talk they did! After everyone reported back, we told them that this event was historically recorded.

Colleagues, if you have never had the privilege of studying the life and times of Moses, who is considered the greatest of prophets in the Old Testament; you are in for a rare treat. At age 80, he was summoned to climb a mountain and eventually lead his people out of Egypt into the "Promised Land". He was a great emancipator who also struggled greatly with speech challenges.

Following our exercise, we esteemed them for not only their rigorous work over the years, but for their upright walk in the world. We spoke about the power that they have to reach our younger men. We expressed to them that men and boys today need lighthouses not outhouses to help them on their journey. As mothers of boys, we pleaded with them to take the dynamic role of a "mentor of men". When we left, we both realized that by far, this was the most exhilarating experience in our professional lives, period!

Powersources are also those who not only help you in desperate times, they can act as a visionary in crafting your purpose. Ask your powersources these questions, "You know me really well, what do you see me doing with my life, given my painful past? What are my strengths and weaknesses? What do you see as my gifts? What things do you think will cause me to stumble on my path to finding purpose? Can you help me see the positive that can come about with all of my pain?" You will probably be amazed at how much they know you and your abilities as well as areas needing intervention. A word of caution though; you may not like some of their remarks because your heart has not prepared itself for what could be a direct discourse. Be willing to keep an open mind. Remember, an open mind is a gold mine.

Here is a concept that may seem rather foreign. We can learn some of our most powerful lessons from someone much younger. Go figure! As parents of young adults (tantalizing teens that is), we can certainly attest to the many times that our children have enlightened us. In many ways, they are like "cognitive Correctol"! The brutal honesty that flows from their mouth is quite astounding. Children, especially teenagers, are gatekeepers for adult accountability, especially when we veer off to the right or left just a little! The old cliché that ***children are to be seen and not heard*** is just so wrong. Consider the integrity of the Native American family. As we mentioned early on, we continue to provide professional development to First Nation's teachers, staff, parents, and students. We have sat with parents inviting them to share their intimate stories and traditions of family. They continually disclose how ***essential*** children are to their family and extended family. Within many indigenous populations, ***extended family means family***! One such woman is Elizabeth's sister-in-law, Wileen Whipple Johnson, mother of three children and a Lakota Sioux from South Dakota. While having lunch with Wileen and her four year old son, Wyatt, we discussed this particular Native tradition. Wileen told us that children are highly esteemed because they carry forth the rich traditions. Children are to be ***seen and heard*** continually even at the expense of adult conversation. We personally evidenced this in Wyatt's demeanor and his strong desire to be an integral part of our adult conversation—continuously! He was an active participant within our discourse. Wow, may the seeds of our indigenous people continue to sew the fabric of our nation's families. Don't think for a moment that being an adult means that we cannot receive nuggets of wisdom from the youth in this world.

To close out this entity called powersources, there is one more reality that we must deal directly with. It can be quite a painful one, too. It deals with those people who have been instrumental in turning-your-world upside down—they are destroyers not builders of humanity! You know fully well that these individuals have NOT been powersources; rather they have created destructive brown-outs and power outages! These human beings (those struggling with ***unattended*** human frailty) have shut down the power and potential of our person. They are life-takers and have left us feeling powerless and thoroughly drained. Yet, can their negative contributions serve the greater good? Is it possible that every seed of adversity can grow an equal and equivalent harvest? It's that whole Ying-Yang thing! What influence have these negative power-outage-people had on you? Can we take the negative influences and transform them into positive outcomes? When one can take the negative and sift-out the positive, it diffuses resentment. Wasn't it Charles Dickens that said, "It was the best of times . . . It was the worst of times"? His famous book, *A Tale of Two Cities*, evidences many brutal paradoxes in life as well as ways to germinate purpose. The hidden undertones of his discourse can act as a vehicle for finding the positive hidden within the negative. This can be a very empowering exercise. We challenge you to record your reflections. Could it be possible that we can pick up some *nuggets of knowledge* from seemingly destructive encounters? Challenge yourself to think beyond the obvious. Finally, think about why destructive individuals behave the way they do. There is something to gather from everyone in our lives. What do we do if we find ourselves with a wounded, angry, and fearful heart? We have a choice to make. Remember, it is all about how we walk through the journey. We cannot control what happens to us, be we do hold the reigns on how we proceed.

The last entity within the "Place of Further Still" and one that will assist in illuminating our purpose is that of "PASSION". Again, let's revisit the Greek lexicon for its historical usage and underpinnings. Etymologically, the term *passion* is a very, very old term and has virtually lost its original intent. Today, due to dictionary evolution (bah-humbug) and the seemingly moral decay of our nation, it has taken on a sexual connotation. How tragic. When researching its original usage, meaning, and progression, it is necessary to examine many dictionaries over time—a longitudinal analysis. It was and continues to be an exciting adventure to be able to search the origin and progression of words and how they flirt with language.

When "passion" is used as a noun, it means *a suffering or passive emotion*. Passion used as an adjective, references *like feelings or affections.* Our research chronicles the progression of the term and cites it's early and first usages. Interestingly enough, passion does not refer to one's physical pain; it infers great emotional pain or spiritual pain. To further deconstruct the term, we find references that catalog passion in a twofold manner.

First, it evidences our commitment to something or someone who is in pain (hence—our students, families, colleagues). Second, our passion foretells our strong feelings or preferences. This alludes to our inherent gifts, skills, desires, and talents (both nature and nurture). Simplistically, it's those things that we do and do WELL. It's those things that we feel and feel profoundly. Many of you might have taken a personality inventory test or gifts revealer analysis. Were you able to see and verify your talents and skills? Did the test reveal specific strengths and identified weaknesses or areas of improvement? You may have found out that you greatly excel in organization or in offering hospitality. You might have been enlightened to the fact that you have great listening/auditory skills necessary to help others discern. Or, you may have had the affirmation that you cannot stand to be in a position without freedom. Are you a people-person or enjoy working solo?

The following represent Elizabeth's gifts and populations that she is in great pain for that was illuminated from several personality inventories and in conversations with her mentors.

Passions
- Spontaneity
- Freedom
- Teaching
- Mission-Centered
- Students in Crisis
- Homeless Families
- Adopted Children

As you can easily ascertain from Elizabeth's bullet pointing, her pain, powersources and passions align perfectly. In completing this exercise, you will begin to see themes and patterns that will begin to illuminate your purpose and an unveiling of your calling. Remember, it takes time and continuous contemplation as to what lies ahead for those who are willing to seek-out the ungroomed path never traveled. Pain, powersources, and our passions are forecasters and crafters of our purpose. Purpose is a welcomed guest; one that invites meaning into our lives. Purpose is the sounding bugle that announces and summons our calling.

Located within one's "Place of Further Still" is where passion seizes permanent residence. Our passions (the gifts that we use to help others in great pain) can take us to new heights IF we take the time to contemplate them and catapult them into action. (Here we go again . . . the dynamic duo called action and contemplation strikes again!) When we move teachers through the process of discovering purpose we suggest to them that their passion ignites their internal combustion components. It energizes and brings to the forefront our deeply held motivations. Passion is a ***gifts revealer*** and invigorates one to the core! It informs the heart and feeds the soul.

We happened to be sitting in a waiting room when we saw a young nine year old girl writing what appeared to be poetry and drawing elaborate pictures of women's formal clothing. She seemed to elicit an amazing zeal for her work. She noticed that we were staring at her notebook and commenting on her tenacity. We asked her to describe the figure that she was drawing? She said that she and her sister (who was 17 months old) were going to be fashion designers in a big city someday. We looked over at her little sister and she was quietly sucking on a bottle of milk! Without giving a definition, we asked her to tell us what the word "passion" meant to her. She turned to her notebook and wrote the following note to us. She wrote, ***"What's more than a girl's passion without a dream? Your dreams can't come true without a heart deep down in the future. When your heart is going your passions are your truths!"*** Wow! Her name is Emajae and she is a stellar artist and student at a school in Ypsilanti, Michigan. So if any of you are wondering what you can learn from a nine year old—here you go! Remember this old saying . . . "and the youth shall lead them". Thanks Emajae, we will look for your designer clothing line in stores everywhere in about twenty years or so! Go, Girl! Clearly, she is a powersource for her parents and friends.

Now, looking at the third "P" on your paper, write the word 'PASSION' and underneath that word, respond to the following questions. What are you passionate about? This means, what are the things that you are willing to go to the mat for? What things convict your heart and drive your actions? Are you into supporting any causes? Are there any hot spots that absolutely drive you bonkers? What are some of your gifts and talents that will help make your life more meaningful? Your answers should be very, very revealing. Now let's put this whole thing together!

As previously stated, the 3 P's---Pain, Powersources and Passion inform and support our calling, driven by our purpose. Let's quickly revisit the three "Ps". Pain within our life can be, by far, the greatest predictor of purpose. Powersources are those individuals and convictions that offer us vision and hope. They act much like a safety net as we embark upon the tightrope called LIFE. Powersources are our mentors and those whose lives are marinated in severe stewardship. They are compassionate truth-tellers. Our passion encompasses all of our gifts, talents, and skills that have been crafted within our DNA and hopefully manifested and nurtured within our environment. Remember . . . discovering purpose is a process that is not able to be rushed or artificially manufactured. Accelerating purpose is much like rushing into a clothing store **blindfolded** and randomly pulling an outfit off the rack and purchasing it void of trying it on.

In closing, we hold fast to our strong biases regarding the dynamic adventure awaiting the discovery of one's life purpose and subsequent calling. We have compiled some "reality checks" as touch points for your contemplation. Although this book lends itself to purposeful teaching, your individual calling may be something other than education and that is tremendous. After all, there are many ways to baste a turkey! Regardless of where one is called (their mission field) those who discover purpose will see that the CALLED have both an individual and corporate purpose. The following represents the commonalities inherent in our answering the call to serve. These check points can be utilized regardless of what calling you have. As you will certainly see, there is no room for the self-centered, the self-immersed, or for the prideful. There are light years between pride and humility and even greater distance between worldly success and stewardship.

Check ✓ ✓ ✓ ✓ this out (pun intended):

REALITY CHECKS

✓ Our own beliefs about purpose lie at the very heart of our behaviors.

✓ A wounded, angry, or bitter heart yields an unleavened purpose.

✓ Power and fear, mixed with self-pity, drive self-serving behaviors.

✓ A joyful heart yields a purpose and is not life taking. It's one that clearly discerns the difference between making a living and making a life, between serving self and serving others.

✓ Joyful purposeful serving transforms one's "power" to "empower". It never usurps another's power.

And now for the BIG reality check . .

.

Our Purpose IS the People We Serve!

Food for thought . . .

*"I don't know what your destiny will be, but one thing
I do know, the only ones among you who will be really
happy are those who have sought and found how to serve."*
----Albert Schweitzer

> *"It is in giving that we receive."*
> -----St. Francis of Assisi

> *"To rule truly is to serve."*
> ----I Ching

> *"An individual has not started living until he can rise
> above the narrow confines of his individualistic concerns to the
> broader concerns of all humanity."*
> ----Dr. Martin Luther King, Jr.

> *"No grief, pain, misfortune, or broken heart
> is an excuse for cutting off one's life..."*
> ---Charlotte Perkins Gilman

> *"Service is what life is all about."*
> ---Marian Wright Edelman

> *"Anyone who devotes himself to the cultivation on his
> own case will become a selfish pig."*
> ---Woodrow Wilson

> *"There is no greater calling than to serve your fellow
> man."*
> ---Walter Ruether

"You may be exhausted with work, even kill yourself, but unless your work is interwoven with love it is useless." (a humble teacher)

We ask that you take a moment and reflect upon this quote. Can you guess whose words they reflect? Clearly, this quote reflects a life full of both contemplation and action. This stellar individual is actually very well known to almost every American; she is an international icon. Just as food is required for sustaining our life, so is the power of love that she shed for people. Amazingly, people enter and profoundly impact our lives either personally or from a distance. Whether near or far away, they have the potential to sculpt our choices and decisions in ways we never fathomed.

She was and continues to be a real ***powersource***. You see, our powersources walk more than they talk! Their words are minimal and their walk packs a punch. Sometimes the words that they speak, or the things they model, don't POWERPACK us until their life is swept away from us. Sadly, during the upcoming moments without them, we find ourselves clinging-on-to the memories. These gentle giants may be totally different than we are or possess a frightening mirror image.

The story below is about a very special, yet simple teacher; one who has touched a multitude of lives in professional and personal ways. She is still referred to as "the most powerful woman in the world". The profound joy of her heart is like a magnet that attracts us. The simplicity of her life provided her with great inspiration and perseverance. Throughout her early training and unfolding of her calling, she awaited patiently for her life's purpose to be illuminated. After all, a heart filled with passion never gives up.

Born Agnes Gonxha Bojaxhiu, she lived a contemplative life within a chaotic world of action and reaction. She was involved within many aspects of her community. At age 9, (much like our young designer, Emajae) she was being groomed for a unique calling. Agnes lost her father during the ninth year of her life, but seemed undeterred in her path to find purpose and meaning. Many young girls would be completely devastated at the loss of their father, but Agnes seemed even more determined! At age 12, she intensely felt a call into a missionary life. Her passion guided her heart in the direction of serving those in pain, especially those who were impoverished. She was intent on never allowing poor people to go empty handed or empty-stomached!

While most 18 year olds are dreaming of their own life and potential success (whatever that means), Agnes was envisioning and meditating on how she could impact the lives of others. She stated, "I am called to help the individual, to love each poor person." This intense selflessness and sweet humility drew her to a pious life to be shared with a group of other young like-minded women. She took her religious vows and eventually became a nun in India. Her new name was Sister Teresa. Her order entitled, "The Sisters of Loreto", were highly devoted to teaching. Her first assignment was that of a geography and history teacher, while dedicating her life to education. This dedication grew into a leadership role; that of a school principal. While serving as an educator, her life's calling was mightily unfolding. She recalls that teaching was her devotion, but serving the poor her vocation.

It was on personal declaration of serving the poor upon which she founded "The Missionaries of Charity", an order dedicated to that cause. She then became known to the world as "Mother Theresa". Let us, as educators, not get caught up in the fact that she carried a particular religious banner; rather let us get caught up in the heart and character that she modeled for billions of people. A woman, who had so little, had so much. The little that she did have was shared by all. In many ways, she modeled that "less is more". She was not selfish, but selfless; a life foreign to many. She gave all she had, which was love in action. Teresa was a woman who, from as early as 12 year's old, endured great **pain**, utilized her monumental **powersources**, and heeded her **passion**. These informed her purpose. From teacher to humanitarian; a call within a call, Mother Teresa was successful (and now we know what that means)! Nothing more needs to be said about a human being that stands revered by humankind. According to biographer, Jean Maalouf, "The story of Mother Teresa has and continues to be called the most revered and the most powerful woman in the world." She clearly negotiated her life work in the intersection where content meets the human condition.

What a quintessential, captivating example of answering and heeding the call to serve! Her words were simple, almost child-like and her work conveyed a captivating yet alarming sense of urgency. Our departed colleague, Mother Theresa (a teacher, principal, and humanitarian) was immersed in a life of stewardship and she didn't only leave a legacy, she lived a legacy.

Chapter 4
"We've Gotta Reach Em' to Teach Em':
"The Character of The Called"

     Entrance into this chapter will grapple with two riveting questions . . . ones that will rightly divide those who are called to teach and those who view teaching as *just* another job. The first question very simply is, *"If teaching is much more than just a 'job' then what is it (an inner power or gut-wrenching spiritual force) that summons one to the teaching trenches?"* What does the phrase "called to teach" really infer? Furthermore, the next query will serve as a wake-up call and sobering indicator as to the *authenticity* of one's call to teach. It is crafted to separate the heavy cream from the powdered Cremora. Ready?

"What does is mean to teach at the intersection where content and delivery meets the fragile human condition?"

Whoa, this is a question worthy of pondering. This is the very same insightful inquiry that our first chapters have grappled with. May we now be so bold (and admittedly with no humility) to state the following . . . THE ABOVE QUESTION CAN REALLY ONLY BE ANSWERED BY THOSE WHO ARE CALLED TO TEACH! One who has selected teaching from a vending machine or after playing "rock—paper—scissors", may find it utterly frustrating to conjecture a response to this inquiry. Others may even get angry, intimated, or explosively defensive when asked to respond while a select few wonder what the human condition has to do with teaching anyway. How S C A R Y is that???

     Allow us now to embark upon laying a beginning platform upon which to build the premise entitled, *"called to teach"*. After all, brick and mortar void of a foundation, is futile (if you don't believe this . . . ask a builder)! As educators, discriminating a

"CALL" from just a *desire* to teach is absolutely critical. After all, there is a vast difference between receiving a telephone call from a telemarketer and a 911 appeal!   Receiving a teaching call is a *spiritual 911 summons* to the mission field called the classroom. Let's begin our discernment journey by examining a rather recognizable scenario—one that is familiar to many chalk-holders!

"The scene is strangely reminiscent of a typical race day at the 'Kentucky Derby'. An uncontrollable mob of hormone-infested bodies are strained forward with legs stomping and crushing the ground with the anticipation of the ringing of the school bell. This particular school bell is attached to a very old building which houses an alternative middle school located within the heart of a very poor, high crime urban area. When the bell sounds, these bodies instantaneously explode with rabid enthusiasm and uncontested energy as though released from a lifetime of captivity. This is the scene every morning as some 50 previously-expelled adolescents wait impatiently while engaging in chain smoking, profanity, pre-meditated bullying, fighting, and mesmerized interactions with their I-pods, boom-boxes, sweethearts, and cell phones. The well-deserved reputation of these aspiring "drop outs" send lightening-bolt shivers down the weary spine of even the most seasoned and courageous teacher. The new principal, a previous gym teacher within the school, sits silently at her desk staring out the window wondering how she is going to fill several teaching positions. Only last week, she lost three new teachers to 'burn-out' and it is only the third week of the school year!"

Hummm . . . We would like for you to stop, think and deconstruct what you have just read. Carefully and thoroughly ponder upon this scenario for just a moment. Allow us to help you build a pictorial foundation for this situation. Begin by perceiving what the school grounds might look like. Do you envision a well-manicured lawn with eye-appealing landscape? What about the structure of the building? How old would you say that it is? Can you visualize the classrooms, halls, teachers' lounge, bathrooms, and gymnasium? What do you perceive as the students' dispositions, their yearnings, and readiness for learning? Will these young teens seek to transform the current state of our human pain by feverously working toward the common good? Or, do you view this building as a so-called ***adolescent holding-tank*** and as a broken down dumpsite that should be leveled? Picture the teachers, too; what are they like? Do they evidence great, joy, exuberance, and purposeful teaching? What about the parents . . . the community. . . and the individual neighborhoods? Has the whole village surrounding this school made a solemn promise to raise these children? What do you, as an educator, ***really*** envision as you contemplate this scenario? Since no one can, with great legitimacy, read your innermost thoughts, please answer the following questions with the utmost integrity. Through vigorous reflection, allow the ***judge and jury of your heart*** to respond truthfully.

      Upon reading this scenario, did you immediately feel invigorated, professionally-challenged, emotionally-charged, and most of all, pedagogically-aroused? Did you immediately retreat to your "Place of Further Still" to refuel for the societal war against our children and families? Or, did you get a real sense of being thoroughly mentally-exhausted? Did you offer-up a deep sigh of relief and performed ritualistic sacrifices to the teaching gods praying that you will NEVER be assigned to teach in a hell-hole similar to this one? Do you find yourself mentally disfigured and horrified at what you believe are aspiring ***little juvenile delinquents***? Do you feel compelled to cast blame at the responsible parties, e.g., parents, principal, teachers, or anyone that would condone a school like this? Did you feel like an angry taxpayer? More profoundly . . . Did you ignore the silent

suffering inherent in each of the children? Do you really care?
More importantly, did/do you view these students as savages and
potential criminals who you feel greatly relish-in the destruction
of both property and people? And . . . be completely honest now
. . . upon first reading this scenario, did you picture the students
as invaluable and desirable children who (with intense mentoring,
unconditional love, and fervent guidance) hold immeasurable
possibilities? Are the students who await the sounding of this
school bell really capable of becoming Rhode Scholars or are they
becoming a different Roads-Scholar called life's losers?

        As an educator, do you truly see yourself as one who would
be zealous in casting a vision for them well beyond the sun-burned
horizons that char your face? As a teacher, would you consider it
a grand honor and most humble privilege to call them *your kids*?
Would you consider it pure joy our brethren to humbly serve them
and the families that greatly struggle, yet love them profoundly?
Most importantly, when you reviewed this scenario, do you see
HOPE or HELL or both? Candid answers to these questions will
serve as an impetus for beginning to respond to the question, "Am
I really called to be a teacher?"

        *Those pedagogically-endowed possess a moral and
humane conviction, an ethical manifesto about the malleable,
brittle nature of every student REGARDLESS of the verdict
that society has brutally proclaimed. The art of teaching is
the fine art of being fully human. Human frailty encompasses
and manifests every emotion, thought, sensation and act. As
creatures of humanity, we exemplify extreme polarity ranging
from complete human derailment (torture and genocide) to
preeminent agape love (unconditional, volitional, universal,
self-sacrificing, non-discriminating and unwavering)). These
authors-of-possibilities are those who possess an extreme
yearning and remarkable compassion that longs desperately to
help the other. Their hunger emerges from one's innermost core
of "The Place of Further Still".*

        There are those who are called into teaching to serve *specific* populations of students e.g., preschool, elementary, emotionally-impaired, collegiate, religious, high school, private education, home-school, alternative settings, etc. If you were NOT called to teach middle school students within this very diverse alternative setting, this scenario might not *spark your fancy*, yet you would remain a kindred spirit in the fight against societal inequities (alarmingly evidenced within the scenario). You would have immediately viewed this situation as one marinated in both HOPE and HELL as well as one pregnant with possibilities. Regardless of the severity of needs that the students exemplified, your vision for them was undeterred. As you were reading, you excitedly viewed them as children capable of germinating seeds of compassion within others. Those who *are-the-called* also comprehend that within this alternative context, the teacher has the potential to be the greatest of learner! In other words, one whom is called into teaching possesses a character rich in astonishing dispositions that vastly sets them apart from just another *Joe-Shmo Teacher*. The line of demarcation is clearly drawn. Upon which side do you find yourself—the optimist or the pessimist—the dream-creator or dream-squashier—the hopeful or hopeless—a life-giver or life-taker?

Is there an archetypal model . . . a template . . . a prototype . . . a paragon of pedagogy which serves to set the bar for what it means to teach? In other words, is it possible to set forth a template upon which to build a master teacher—one whose character and caricature artfully connects the content within the context of the human condition? Building a seasoned teacher is about constructing the heart of the teacher and of those who are "the taught". The life of the heart of both continues to be a mystery. With every breath we take, we exhale into an unseen direction where we are working to unlock those mysteries. In other words, the pedagogy of one who is driven to teach--*teaches to the heart of the child*.

We believe that there is a model set forth for the creation of a master teacher. There is a rather contagious set of teaching dispositions inherent within the *quintessential model of a teacher*. By outlining these dispositions we do not seek to destroy an educator's creativity and bent on teaching. We respectfully acknowledge and embrace diverse/unique teaching styles. Those answering the call to teach DO evidence unbelievable similarities in their pedagogical prowess. Yet, in the context of their vast differences and backgrounds, there are mysterious parallels worthy of examination. It's with great humility and excitement that we reveal the extraordinary likenesses inherent in both the character and caricature that embodies *one whom is called to teach.* Furthermore, our beginning question, "If teaching is much more than just a 'job' then what is it (an inner power or gut-wrenching spiritual force) that summons one to the teaching trenches", is designed to cause each of us to stop dead-in-our-tracks. More than likely our readers will find themselves in one of two categories. First, there are those who will quietly nod their head and softly say, "Yea, this stuff makes total sense to me . . . this resonates with my soul." Second, there are those who may experience an unrest or dissonance with the "aura" of one who is pedagogically-called. Hopefully, after much contemplation, we ALL will broadcast, "Wow, I want to be just like that!" Like what . . . you might ask? Let's find out . . .

To begin with, every school year/semester, we walk into a classroom with great diversity staring back at us. We look into the eyes of a multitude of students who have issues, problems, gifts, and various baggages. Teachers are responsible for bringing forth content aligned to the benchmarks and standards, as well as creating life long learners. How can this be masterfully done with so many minds challenging our paradigms and pedagogy? How can we "REACH EM' TO TEACH EM'?" The answer is within the character and caricature of the teacher. Let us begin by first exploring the concept "character".

According to the *Oxford English Dictionary* (OED), the term "character" implies *one who has distinctive markings and one who possesses the sum of moral and mental qualities.* The "quintessential teacher" possesses specific dispositions that testifies and affirms to her/his calling. These unique markings are the footprints of the character of one destined to prepare students to impact generations. The following reflected the complex simplicities and commonalities that we have witnessed within those who we believe have greatly answered the call to teach.

- ***Their Chalk, Talk, and Walk Are Congruent.*** What they say and do is one-in-the-same. The message and messenger are inseparable. Furthermore, their walk and talk know each other well and one never is out-of-sync with the other. Their teaching conforms to the practicality inherent within human fragility. Everything is contextualized— even context! (Huh?—this may take a little time to comprehend*)* Within this realm, they believe that there is no room for mistruths, misconceptions, and falsehoods. They believe that empowerment is the greatest enforcer of human freedom. Every thought, word, and deed is held captive by every student. EVERY moment is a teachable and reachable moment within their classroom. They place no distance between knowing and doing (contemplation and action). They believe ***that to know*** and ***not to do*** is ***not to know at all***. Knowing is reinforced by doing and showing. Everything lesson ends in praxis. They ARE what they teach. And, they teach what they are. No inconsistencies. They believe clearly that every student placed in their classroom is meant to be there. There are no accidents, just preordained possibilities.

- ***Reality NOT Ritual-Based Lessons.*** Our ***teaching icons*** deduce that experience is our greatest teacher because (as we previously declared) it gives life's tests first and the hard lessons of life learned second. Every lesson is hand-tooled and carefully chosen to meet the demands of the situation in orchestration with the intimate needs of the learner. Each lesson finds solace and resonates within the demands with the core curriculum. The ***called one*** carefully crafts lessons that are never repetitive and verbatim because they realize that students change and grow. The content and concepts may be quite similar, but the delivery is contingent upon those who are the recipients of the delivered goods. They know that failure is an opportunity for communication rather than excommunication! They acknowledge that each student (regardless of their age) lives a "reality TV" life in which the only constant is pain. They believe that every classroom is ripe with diversity and each must struggle with the realities of their own human frailty. Alternative subjects (called heart-core curriculum) such as rejection, failure, disease, poor self image, fear, dreams, love, death, drugs, friends, alcohol, addiction etc., are ones that have the potential to permeate a student's life before the core curriculum is even revealed. They never run from the battle called life. They are careful to weave heart-core concepts into the content and have zero trouble aligning anything to a standard, benchmark, or assessment. You will NEVER hear this pierce their lips, "Hey, take this down because someday you will use this" OR "You're gonna have to learn this cause it's on the test!" Every minute piece of content is marinated in the fragility of the human condition and finds residence within the heart of every student. Again, their *art of affect* leads and informs their cognitive/ academic constructs. They believe that traditional subjects allow the student to splash in the water whereas heart-core curriculum gives them the tools to swim. Lastly, everything they teach is encapsulated within the contexts of extreme contemplation and action (praxis). Preparing students for stewardship is the underground railroad that energizes and drives their pedagogy as well as the power of their person. Their ideas birth pure perspectives on reality rather than condomized (safe) curriculum. In other words, they don't practice safe text!

- ***They Are Relational***! These ***masters-of-the-chalks*** know that their greatest transmitters for truth are relationships. They begin each day by greeting every student, parent, and visitor at the door. They end each day by doing the same. They shake theirs hands and give them HIGH 5's continuously. They carefully embrace their students when their needs are the greatest. They weep with them when the times appear the bleakest. They belly-laugh with them, show an unrelenting reverence for them and their families, attend their places of worship, obnoxiously cheer-lead for them at sporting events, slip them money when they have none, deliver bags of groceries to their home anonymously when their refrigerator and wallets are empty, pray for them and with them regardless of their faith/denomination, counsel them, admit to their personal weaknesses and shortcomings, eat lunch beside them in the cafeteria, attend celebrations with them, shoot baskets and challenge them on the basketball court, have bubble blowing contests, come alongside them when they are in trouble, advocate for them in all instances, reproof them, sing/rap with them, and realize that each of them are to be highly honored and esteemed REGARDLESS . . . These **fighters of families** love unceasingly and unconditionally. **Called teachers** have endless energy and find strength in loving others. There is also a well-defined, healthy relationship between the teacher and the students. There is an unspoken hierarchy and level of respect. **Chalk preachers** invariably focus upon a student's personal needs first at the deepest and most profound of level. They do not pry or gossip. Their word is a covenant never to be broken. They are greatly sympathetic and go out of their way to reprove bigotry. Their relationships model patience, loyalty, meekness and gentleness. They take a student's greatest weakness and make it their greatest strength. They have crafted a vision for each student and do not believe that students have deficits only surplus yet to unleash. They believe in the

integrity, value, and worth of every individual regardless .
.. Lastly . . . THEY SEEK TO UNDERSTAND RATHER
THAN BE UNDERSTOOD!

- ***Illuminators Of The Mind.*** Those ***called to inform***
transcend rigid content dictators—they are mind
emancipators! They are ***extreme exponents*** of their
art. They are great illuminators of the mind and heart.
Their instructional techniques move well beyond a text,
worksheet, ditto, overhead, and computer. They advocate
that the mind is the greatest technological tool yet to
be fully realized. A mind, they broadcast, is a terrible
thing to waste! ***Genuine illuminators*** empower learning
through their usage of concrete pictures and vivid scenes.
Meaningless abstract phrases and acontextualized facts
are enemies of the mind. They use questions that have no
quick answers but engender critical, intense thought. A
carefully crafted question, they believe, has the potential to
permeate a student's thought pattern for a lifetime. They
love the cognitive sport of mental gymnastics and have
earned a varsity letter within this domain! They also speak
using paradoxes, stories, parables, and multiple figures of
speech in the context of diverse points-of-view. Their Ying
continues to Yang! They model cognitive martial arts and
by the end of the year EVERY student has earned a black
belt in thinking outside of any box! Every illumination is
driven by a problem/issue/concern that holds the human
condition hostage. ***Chalksters*** believe there are many
"better" ways, but no one BEST way. Their classroom
discourses resides in "The Place of Further Still" and they
aspire to help students fully comprehend the "workings of
their own mind". These ***beacons-of-light*** use extraordinary
means to excite, ignite, and to get-at-the-core of the heart
curriculum. They meet a student's life demands through
teaching and modeling contemplation, action and extreme
problem solving. Their pedagogy provides not merely

information, but transformation of one's mind through an exploration of the human potential. They believe that the mind is not a storehouse but an instrument to be used and infused.

- ***Knows No Neutrality!*** Our ***non-fence-sitters*** challenge every thought, idea, and construct by taking an ardent stand. They model humility within extreme positionality and are adamant to flush out and discern curricular racism, pomposity, insincerity and pride. They are ***equity-dwellers*** who embrace diverse, especially radical points-of-view. They'd rather be HOT or COLD but never lukewarm or frigid. Debate, justify, articulate, ponder, conceptualize, testify, simplify, calculate, decipher, argue, contemplate, and discern (all in the context of praxis) are common instructional commands. Mediocre and so-so are foreign to their classrooms. These ***mind-circumcisers*** are enthusiastic for insight and change and their classroom is never sterile-- NO rubber gloves are needed here! Social justice permeates their learning environment while sentimental slush is appalling and off limits. Equity will no longer be a silent sledgehammer as far as they are concerned. Democracy, and all that it encompasses, is the reverberating gavel and great emancipator permeating classroom discourse.

- ***Nonjudgmental And Casts No Boulders.*** Acceptance-of-difference is their trademark of teaching underwritten by a selfless motive called affirmation! Those ***majestically-crafted*** are lighthouses, not courthouses, for all students, especially for those who are maligned as classroom cast-aways. Society continues to drive a stake through the hearts of those whom it has labeled as life's losers e.g., the dropouts, rebels, deviants, homely, hurting, helpless, emotionally-challenged, intolerable, poor, underachiev-ers, peculiar, and the disabled. Acceptance, celebration of uniqueness and embracing of extreme difference is the mortar and brick that provides a foundation for their character. These ***men and women of the cause*** are not concerned about their reputation but their responsibility to model compassion void of judgment and finger pointing. They never find fault in one's failure but seek to offer hope and direction to those held captive by a brutal, judgmental world. They move their victimized students from war to inner peace . . . from simple to the profound . . . from self-hate to love of self. They teach the downtrodden to sing sonnets of the heart that lay dormant beneath a societal blanket of injustice. They model and advocate a turning-of-the-cheek, rather than a bruising of another's physique. These individuals move students from emotional exhaustion to mental exhilaration. They see severely marginalized students with an entirely radicalized set of lenses; that is eyes to see the great potential in ALL students REGARDLESS . . . Lastly, they have no desire for power, yet have every motive to empower. They believe that those who have the most power never need to show it!

- ***Predictable Yet Unpredictable.*** Those answering the ***miraculous call to teach*** have a walk in the world (character) that is highly predictable and a pedagogy that is outrageously-unpredictable. Regardless of the setting that you observe them within, their stellar moral and ethical character abounds. Their character-walk mimics those that we will speak about in the last chapter in which we characterize "superheroes". Their absolute honesty, truthfulness and humble disposition are incredibly interwoven with radical teaching strategies that keep their students on the edge of their seats! These ***moral ninjas*** are "edutainers" who use any means by which to allure, stimulate, inspire, and educate. (We will speak more about this later in this chapter).

- *A Master Of Their Content.* These *artful scholars* are tenacious in acquiring the depth and breadth of their content and subject matter. They are continual readers and knowledge-pursuers and will not rest if there is new, groundbreaking content yet to be unearthed. The set the standard for toil. They continually pursue educational journals and research while burning-the-candles keeping updated on new methodologies and innovations within their discipline. They draw relationships between other disciplines—they are *interdisciplinary gurus*! They examine their content using a diverse and fresh-set-of-eyes almost daily. Their exhaustive effort on keeping current provides an exemplary model for life-long learning. They are a learner-first and teacher-second. They continue to weave their data findings within their discourse, instruction, and assessment. These folks believe that they will never achieve content mastery but are always upon a developmental pathway to greater learning. They are kings and queens of content and humble servants of delivery!

- *A Social Visionary.* These *20-20 Oculars* are ones whose vision possesses transparency in foresight and hindsight! They create a wild adventure for every individual who enters their classroom. They envision rather than tunnel-vision. They dream rather than scream. While many sleepwalk through their existence, these cutting edge *storm-troopers* dream beyond the extreme. Their only limits are the limitless. They picture a world free of pain and intolerance while they invent entirely new ways of organizing human effort. They believe in possibilities rather than limitations. They light fires in minds rather than extinguishing them. They make waves and build bridges. These *overseers* also illuminate many pathways for their students toward affirming their uniqueness and creativity. Carefully and craftfully they transform dreams into reality.

They structure the life of a student utilizing three strong pillars of strength—*family, student, and teacher.* These *foresight coaches* lend support for designing the vehicle of a student's life with pure fuel (virtue) and a robust engine (steadfast heart). They delight in a long, intense, and well-reasoned disordering of the senses. They thrive on reconstruction. Where Surrealists tried to elevate the dream-state into a higher reality, *visionary social deconstructionists* use all means at their disposal—even at great personal risk. They see well beyond the boundary and limitation of human insight and sight. They have x-ray vision. They endeavor to see the unseen, hear the unheard, feel the untouched, sense the insensible and give voice to the silenced. Their words and messages are within a new discourse, one that exists only within "The Place of Further Still". Society advocates that an effective teacher helps students grow up to become fully independent—one that is *called-to-transform* insists that living a full life means living interdependently and in communion/harmony with the other. The world would have us believe that the-best-of-the-best teachers are the ones who dream of a well-stocked, technological and futuristic classroom. A social visionary utilizes alternative teaching settings such as mountain-tops, a living room, a tree house, a path, a farm, a churning river, a simple coffee shop, or even a small fishing boat. They believe that the future can artfully reopen the past and unveil authentic instructional tools that have gone by the way side such as the animals, a forest, a wagon, a bottle, some yarn, toys, paint, and nature. Nature is our greatest visionary, our most accomplished scholar, and exemplary teacher in that it manifests the simple sweetness embedded in life; and that, colleagues, is what our dreams should be made of.

Chapter 4.5
"Moving Students from Boredom to Stardom: The Caricature of the Called"

"If the definition of learning is applied knowledge, what learnings are your students currently showing you by how they choose to live their lives? What are you teaching them . . . Spirit Whisperers are 'way showers'... They show us that real education has nothing to do with covering content, but is now and has always been a drawing out of what already exists within the student rather than a putting-in of what we see as necessary to fill perceived deficiencies."

--Chick Moorman

We attended a state conference for teachers whose students were emotionally-challenged, many well beyond what most educators (even special educators) can fathom. It was at that venue that we heard Chick Moorman speak. His message and book was entitled, ***Spirit Whisperers: Teachers Who Nourish A Child's Spirit.*** His message resonated. Following his talk, it was evident that Spirit Whisperers ***got-it-goin'-on*** and breathe life into our breathless students. As we stated earlier within our text, this book is a testimony to not only what we philosophically believe, but how we pedagogically deliver our beliefs--walkin' and talkin' our love child, which is teaching! Does that mean that we think that we are ***all-that***? Absolutely not!! Does that mean that we hold the key to the frustration box of teaching ailments and that we have all the answers to every educational dilemma? Not in the least! Does it mean that we think teaching is ALL THAT? Yep!

We simply believe that the ART and science of teaching journeys well beyond the chalkboard and must have a nonstop route to the heart of those under our tutelage. In order for education to be the breath-of-life, it must transcend standards and legislative-dictated assessments. Life curriculum supersedes academic content for those called to teach. It's within the context of life curriculum that academic content is delivered.

We believe that how we deliver the material and how we walk our walk, can make or break the spirit of those we are destined to teach. That is why we are so convicted in bringing forth what we call *the lost art of simplistic teaching*. We want to replenish the supply of joy that is greatly, greatly (did we say GREATLY?) lacking in virtually every classroom and school that we have been invited into. How wonderful would it be if teachers and students wake up every morning rabid (foaming at the mouth) to experience what is in store for them as they team up as a community of learners? You might say that as staff developers, our role is one of "joy artists"! We campaign on behalf of a student's J.Q. (joy quotient) rather than I.Q. (intelligence quotient) which is NOT a testimony to student potential, only a barrier that society has created to sort and select!

To watch your students' dispositions transform into *recipients and activists of joy* nourishes the soul of teacher. A joyful child offers hope to a struggling and fatigued parent. Furthermore, when you witness the metamorphosis from the childhood cocoon to soaring adult, you stand proud and humbled that *just maybe* you had a little bit to do with how far they have come. While participating at this state conference we were pleased to find that one of Elizabeth's former students was the recipient of the "Exceptional Teacher of the Year" award. What a gratifying moment! When her name was announced, we rose with such pride and clapped until our hands were weary and red. You see, she was called into teaching emotionally-challenged adolescents well into her thirties. She went back to school for teacher certification because every time she passed an adolescent rehabilitation center, she KNEW that she was to, one day, be an integral part. SHE KNEW HER PURPOSE and has never felt more fulfilled than she is now with what some view as being *just a teacher.* The scenario that we set before you in the last chapter about the alternative middle school was much like the place that she currently teaches within. You see, she possesses both the character and caricature of one who has been summoned to serve. She is a joy-generator for "her kids". Now lets talk about the classroom and how we can REACH EM' TO TEACH EM' through examining the *caricature* of the called teacher.

When you hear the term "caricature" what images do you conger-up? Do you think of the time that you went to the carnival and had a rather stressful-looking artist draw your portrait? Do you remember sitting there while carnival-attendees walked by you and smirked? Did you notice that upon completion, all of your features (mouth, eyes, nose, legs, chin, etc.) were alarmingly exaggerated? And more frightening, you actually paid hard cash for a humorous rendition of something that didn't even look like you! (Or did it—ugh!) You laid down about $20.00 for something that a 5 year old budding artist might have been able to pull-off! Question--what does "caricature" have to do with someone who has been called to teach? The answer is EVERYTHING. Let us begin by looking at the definition of this term—in other words, W.W.W. S. (What Would Webster Say?)

Webster's Handy College Dictionary describes caricature as *a humorous illustration that exaggerates or distorts the basic essence of a person or thing to create an easily identifiable visual likeness.* In other words, caricature is an assertive act of exaggeration! We think e x a g g e r a t i o n is what instruction should be made of (note the word "eager" found within exaggeration). We think of our *Reach Em' to Teach Em'* strategies as curriculum caricatures borne out of best practice. What happens when something is exaggerated in the context of teaching? An overstimulation of content (exaggeration) breathes life into what a student views as seemingly dead and boring curriculum (curriculum void of the human condition). Sensationalizing content does not infer lying to a student or providing falsehoods of information for the purpose of getting-their-attention. No way! It is a methodolgoy that we use frequently and have found tremendous success and a great increase in student achievement. The caricature of a teacher is also the caricature of one who is also an effective classroom manager. How one orchestrates their classroom is a testimony to what they believe about the human condition. The human condition is all about human interaction and reaction. The setting (classroom environment) should empower the plot (curriculum and instruction)!

Therefore, the greatest classroom management strategy (other than summer ☺) is EFFECTIVE TEACHING!   In other words, teaching with the caricature of one who is sold-out to an environment filled with vibrant communication is one that is purposely exaggerated with meaningful cognition and acute-care compassion.

We are geaked to introduce the concept of *pedagogical caricature* which we fondly refer to as 3-D learning.   3-D (that's D to the 3rd power for you math teachers!) is pedagogy pregnant with drama, distortion, and depth. How many of you recall going to a 3-D movie and as you entered the theatre, the usher handed you a pair of funkie glasses with red celephane lenses. Cool duuude! You sat there, popcorn and coke in hand, and the movie began. From the moment you put on the glasses, large images on the screen leaped-out-at-you and the figures, who seemed almost surreal, came alive as if they were right in front of your face. You found yourself ducking and dodging as items seemed to come right-at-you! It was really quite freaky and it almost seemed like an out-of-body experience! The screen took on a definite new dimension; the traditional theatre with a flat surfaced screen was transformed with depth and breadth. Distortion, drama, and depth inform the art of exaggeration called "caricature". But why go to such extreme measures as a teacher? This is a question that is always asked during many of our professional development workshops. We believe that we have a worthy and invaluable answer. The answer lies beside a rather simple southern catfish pond in Arkansas. Let's take a fishing trip to the wild waters, where ripples move in endless directions, fish jump to catch bait, and a fishergirl sits for hours determining what lure she needs next to hook the BIG fish.

Colleagues, I (Elizabeth) have always loved to fish. Why? Because my dad loved to fish and we would try to get away on the weekends to dip-a-line in many lakes in Lower Michigan. We'd leave mom at home to clean the house and do her thing. We would pack a basket of treats and head out for the old fishin' hole. Dad taught me everything that I know about types of fish, lures, line, reels, rods, and live bait! We fished together for my formative years (and still do on the weekends as much as we can get away to do so). Well, at age 18, I left for college in Arkansas and lived in a dorm near my aunt and uncle in Sedgwick (a really, really small town). Uncle Russ and Aunt Skeet were rice farmers and also farmed catfish! Have you ever heard of that? They designed 3 ponds (small, medium, and larger) that housed various sizes of catfish from tiny to HUGE twenty pounders! They grew the catfish from tiny, tiny almost minnow-sized and upon full growth, would sell them to various companies that marketed fish.

Well, every weekend following my classes, I would escape to the catfish pond to do some serious fishing. I was in my 3rd year at college and getting ready to do my student teaching. Oh, I dreamed of catching THE BIG ONE every time I went to the pond. I can't begin to tell you how wonderful it was watching people sit in their lawn chairs and throw out their line. It was a very sweet time in my life; one that I think about often. It seemed like every elderly person, over age 80, was at my uncle's pond! They were SERIOUS about their fishing, too! One day, I sat there thinking. . . Hum . . . isn't fishing kind of like teaching? Interestingly enough, it was the weekend adventures at the catfish pond that proved to be my greatest teaching methods course! Why?

There are so many different species of fish beneath the surface who share the waters, yet given their similarities (being fish), they all act and react in a very unique way. Consider the simple Sunfish; one that will bite on a small chunk of worm on a very small hook at anytime, day or evening—they are always biting and hungry! They rarely bite on artificial bait. In fact, I have never caught a sunfish on anything other than on a portion of a worm and small hook. You have to use a tiny hook because their mouth is so small. You find them within the first 7 or 9 feet below the surface. What about the Bass (largemouth or smallmouth), and their unique dispositions? They are more intelligent and savvy than the sunfish. Bass are a fisherman's recreational dream. They love to hide and feed near the shore and within weed beds. They don't hang out in deep water. They are pernickety and love to be entertained by different types of lures; usually the ones that have been carefully crafted and designed JUST FOR THEM! They will hit (bite) on nightcrawlers, jigs, Slo-Poke Grubmasters, Junebug Gumbler Sweebo Worm, Alewife Gambler Spinnerbait, and Chartreuse Bait to name only a few dynamite lures. The hooks for bass are larger than that of a sunfish because their mouths are larger and stronger.

And then, how about the catfish—the southern catfish, that has quite a different accent than the Yankee catfish, is a very interesting cat! Catfish grown and farmed down south are very intriguing (as well as UGLY) to say the least. You find them in very muddy water. They hang out at the bottom of a pond. They are very docile and grow quite large. You will need a larger pole, heavy line, and a much larger hook. The bait for catfish can be purchased in large plastic containers and looks much like cookie dough, although smells much like toilet-dough! Ack! You open up the container, grab a larger fingerful of dough, roll it together in a ball and slap it on the hook. Dip the hook in the water to get it cold and then add a sinker to your line so that it will go directly to the bottom where they are waiting for food. I remember making catfish bait with my uncle. He used cat-poop, the fuzzy tops of cattails, aged cheese and oatmeal to hold it together. It worked wonderfully!

Catfish are bottom-feeders—Sunfish are top-feeders—Bass hide in the weeds and reeds and are finicky-eaters! Why doesn't all bait/lures work for all species of fish? Why do some feed just on the bottom, while other runs their mouths on the surface? The answer is the same as to this question, "Why do some children learn best with repetition, lecture, and textbooks, while others need extreme active engagement, song, and dance? The answer is DIFFERENCE! All species of fish come from diverse areas in the pond, live, eat, and have vastly different dispositions, needs, wants, and desires. Teaching is angling. Teachers . . . if you ever go to a fishing store like Gander Mountain or Cabela's, note the multitudes of lures and live bait. There is no one-lure-catches-all! Yes, it would be much more efficient if there was only one lure to snag all fish. It would also be a lot cheaper. Too bad, so sad . . . that's not how it works with fish OR with our students. Hear us now . . .

We begin our "REACH EM' TO TEACH EM" workshop dressed up as fishermen. In our hands we hold a rod and reel. We ask our teachers, "What does a simple fishing pole and hook have to do with teaching and learning?" They immediately say, "We've gotta hook our students"! And we broadcast, "RIGHT ANSWER"! We ask them to consider the ways and means by which they attempt to "hook" them. We suggest to them that teachers have to FIRST affectively hook-them (meaning a student's feelings, values, emotions, desires) in order to reel-them-in cognitively (teacher's academic content)! Next, we ask them why they believe that it is necessary to (much like the angler in pursuit of a particular type of fish) consider specific methodologies (bait/lures) that will be the most effective to hook them (meaning helping them make the decision to learn). They immediately share with us that herein lay the dilemma—their greatest struggle as teachers. In other words, what does it take to Reach-Em' to Teach Em' nowadays? Is it possible for us to return to the *lost art of simplistic teaching;* a time when the sweetness of the simple spoke volumes? A time when the number 9 1 1 meant eleven. Oh well, these times, they are a-changin'! What's it gonna take to reach and teach our babies who live in a society gagged, bound, and held hostage by media influences their pie-crust promises (easily made—easily broken).

What lures can we use as teachers? Let's see.

Comrades . . . fellow called-teachers . . . the following statements may be the most powerful ones within this chapter and have the greatest potential to transform our pedagogical practice.

We, as teachers and parents, are in competition for the hearts and minds of our students. We battle daily with the continual regiment of emotional holocausts permeating children's emotions, feelings, self-efficacy, beliefs, and purpose. Pre-meditated media influences such as M.T.V., American Idol, Fear Factor, B.E.T., I-pods, , MP3's, Cosmopolitan Magazine, Soap Operas, Video Games, Chat Lines, Pornography, Radio Stations, Music, Commercials, Movies, Music Videos, Game Shows, Internet, Web Pages, etc., are only some of the aggressive stimuli that act as a fun house mirror upon which our youth measure their self-worth and self-image. Our youth use this distorted mirror as a means to compromise and justify their decisions. The sobering question is, "Who is really winning the battle—the media or those who greatly care for our youth?" As parents first and teachers second, we wholeheartedly and profoundly believe that we are losing not only the battle, but have the potential to lose the war.

During the Bill Clinton years as president, First Lady Hillary Clinton addressed a nation about the difficulties involved with raising children in context of media influences, parenting, and teaching. She declared on Tuesday, Aug. 27, 1996 that it "Takes a Whole Village to Raise a Child". The following are excerpts from her address.

"Right now, in our biggest cities and our smallest towns, there are boys and girls being tucked gently into bed, and there are boys and girls who have no one to call mom or dad, and no place to call home.

Right now there are mothers and fathers just finishing a long day's work. And there are mothers and fathers just going to work, some to their second or third jobs of the day.

Right now there are parents worrying: "What if the baby sitter is sick tomorrow?" Or: "How can we pay for college this fall?" And right now there are parents despairing about gang members and drug pushers on the corners in their neighborhoods.

Right now there are parents questioning a popular culture that glamorizes sex and violence, smoking and drinking, and teaches children that the logos on their clothes are more valued than the generosity in their hearts.

But also right now there are dedicated teachers preparing their lessons for the new school year. There are volunteers tutoring and coaching children. There are doctors and nurses caring for sick children, police officers working to help kids stay out of trouble and off drugs.

Of course, parents, first and foremost, are responsible for their children.

But we are all responsible for ensuring that children are raised in a nation that doesn't just talk about family values, but acts in ways that values families. Just think - as Christopher Reeve so eloquently reminded us last night, we are all part of one family - the American family. And each one of us has value. Each child who comes into this world should feel special - every boy and every girl.

"IT TAKES A VILLAGE TO RAISE A CHILD"

I chose that old African proverb to title my book because it offers a timeless reminder that children will thrive only if their families thrive and if the whole of society cares enough to provide for them. The sage who first offered that proverb would undoubtedly be bewildered by what constitutes the modern village. In earlier times and places--and until recently in our own culture--the "village" meant an actual geographic place where individuals and families lived and worked together.

For most of us, though, the village doesn't look like that anymore. In fact, it's difficult to paint a picture of the modern village, so frantic and fragmented has much of our culture become. Extended families rarely live in the same town, let alone the same house. In many communities, crime and fear keep us behind locked doors. Where we used to chat with neighbors on stoops and porches, now we watch videos in our darkened living rooms. Instead of strolling down Main Street, we spend hours in automobiles and at anonymous shopping malls. We don't join civic associations, churches, union, political parties, or even bowling leagues the way we used to. . . "

That's right Mrs. Clinton . . . things ain't what they used to be, especially within our modern village. How we wish that we could entrust our children with our society. But, the village in the traditional African proverb, as Mrs. Clinton speaks, "Doesn't look like that anymore." As parents, we don't want the village raising our children!

Our modern village is one marinated in a pop culture that promises our youth that they can have it all, get-rich quick, be a model . . . or just look like one, be the next American Idol, have great sex, be a swinger, why not have a threesome . . . multiple partners. . . get high . . . use a condom and guarantee safe sex, try this cream . . . it eliminates all lines and wrinkles, get a face lift and take 60 years off your looks, have a perfect body, want a stomach with a 6 pack . . . we'll show you how to have great Abs in just 30 short minutes a day. . . lose 100 pounds with no-risk by-pass surgery, lose all your fat with Atkins, or better yet ladies . . . do anything you need to do to have a perfect 10 body e.g., vomit, use enemas, take diuretics, liquid diets, Dexatrim, Slim-Fast, Hollywood Diet, South Beach, carb-blockers, appetite suppressants, Zone diet, low sodium, or be anorexic and look like a model with her new 70 pound sexy, adolescent-looking, boy body—after all, she might be the new Guess model! What do you have to lose????

The answer is . . . your life, your beliefs, your family, your freedom, your health, your savings, your morals, your purpose, your potential, and yourself! Interestingly enough, it's not only our youth that is entangled in the pop culture craze.

Pop culture can be defined as the daily interactions, needs, desires, cultural moments that make up the everyday lives of the mainstream. It is inclusive of any number of practices, including mass media, cooking, clothing, entertainment, sports, and literature. Pop culture within the modern village is inclusive of the provocative stimuli whose visual and auditory containers market pre-meditated, empty guarantees. These nebulous pledges have fermented into mythical, heroic images that are calculated messages to lure and entice us. It is our belief that these modern mythological images that pop culture portrays within one's unconscious mind are raping and seducing our youth and sadly, many adults. Their unfulfilled promises leave a path of devastation and carnage within our youth. The carnage is called pain, hopelessness, and rejection (outcries of our human condition). Why are young adults falling victim to these modern mythological images and how can we, as teachers, respond? Well, when the going gets tough, we teachers are tougher! Where can we turn FELLOW TEACHERS to beat pop culture at its own game? We would like to offer a message of hope and our firm belief as to how we can win the war for our nation's youth—Here we go . . .

"It Takes A Whole Village to Prepare A Teacher!" Say what? Think about it . . . if we as educators clearly understood what was going on in the modern village that was infiltrating the emotional quotient of our kids, we would be greatly armed and prepared to battle those mighty forces and fortress. In fact, the village provides the strongest caricature for our youth! Sadly, as teachers we are at a loss as to how to deal with the power of pop culture. A January 2004 article, appearing in the *Journal of Urban Youth Culture* by Cameron White, presents a mini-manifesto regarding this dilemma. The following are excerpts that support our conviction that we MUST clearly know the obstacles in the village in order to Reach Em' to Teach Em'.

"Our society has made youth culture a cornerstone of cultural identity and we simply cannot ignore that fact. Television, movies, music, and other media provide fodder for connections among our disconnected citizenry. Why not use this rather than belittle it? We owe it to our kids to provide opportunities for critical analysis of youth culture . . . Unfortunately, children experience few opportunities to engage youth culture except outside of school . . . It seems that schools have evolved to places where it is encouraged not to take chances. A standardized curriculum, instruction, and procedures dictate little risk-taking. Teachers and administrators have become afraid to drift from the norm. Teachers often even state that they don't have time to integrate anything but the mandated curriculum. The accountability and achievement movement has severely limited what can occur in schools in the name of teaching and learning. A bland and boring social education has thus emerged . . . Youth culture can counter this negative trend. If we are truly interested in motivating kids to learn and apply this learning to the broader spectrum of social literacy, then we must make stronger efforts at integrating meaningful curriculum and instruction that includes real-world connections. These connections allow kids to develop the scaffolding needed to construct knowledge. Youth culture can enhance a transformative rather than transmissive social education by providing these connections. Youth culture and social efficacy themes can really make a difference for our children in their learning experience. The real question for us is how can we remain complacent if we really do care about our children and their future . . . Creating a world of caring and compassion through social justice requires the cultivation of the human spirit . . . Teachers and others interested in social efficacy approaches in schools must realize that neutrality is an impossibility. What is important is creating a classroom atmosphere where students and teachers are empowered to question and critically analyze . . . It is time to allow the good times to roll in school. Youth culture is a naturally intrinsically motivating factor in our lives and should be integrated into the teaching and learning process in our schools. What better way to engage in critical inquiry and problem solving for social efficacy than use youth culture within our schools?"

What powerful passages! We must equate and relate youth culture, which has become the ***most influential institution*** for children and teens in our society. Youth culture is a mighty informant and can attest to their human condition. A student's natural desire is to make sense of their world and pop culture can be the pedagogical instrument to facilitate this process. Media is the greatest transmission mechanism for pop culture. It craftfully preys upon our youth's non-acceptance of themselves and places an unrealistic standard of bodily perfection, heightened sexual erection, and dysfunctional emotional connection. WHY DON'T WE, AS EDUCATORS, PREY ON POP CULTURE as a means upon which to create connections, acceptance of self and acceptance of difference? Rather than blindly accepting or outright rejecting the "Disneyfication" or "South Parking" that is interfering with the emotions of our children—rather use them as reachable encounters. Using Disney and its animated films such as "Aladdin" or "Pocahontas" to analyze gender and cultural stereotypes, will ignite a rich discourse around the themes of body types, hair color and texture, privilege, ethnicity, racism, etc. Pop and youth culture are intrinsic motivating factors (can't we too, remember back to our youth and what we were into?). We must integrate the power of pop into our institutions of learning—from pre-school to post doctoral levels. David Purpel and Svi Shapiro's text, ***Beyond Liberation and Excellence: Reconstructing the Public Discourse on Education*** sums it up by declaring, "Creating a world of caring and compassion through social justice and youth culture requires the cultivation of the human spirit, the nourishment of the image and the impulse for self-expression."

Teachers, we believe that pop culture is a very powerful and controlling caricature in that it distorts, dramatizes, and deepens (depth) our youth's self-image and self-worth. Within ***this*** context, these 3-D words are not promise-keepers but heart-breakers. That is the very thing that a funhouse mirror does when we stand in front of it—it ***distorts*** our features, changes our ***depth***, and places us within the ***drama*** of a superficial Hollywood life. Pop culture is a funhouse mirror that our youth holds-on-to as a template for their self-image. Poor self-image—poor self-worth; it's that simple. No let's talk about specifics . . . specifically, how CAN we beat pop culture at its own deceptive game?

Teaching is like the "Call of the Wild" and those who may be the most wild might be those who are also eventually called to man-the–chalkboard. Imagine if Rapper Eminem were called into teaching! Crazier things have happened. Let's now move to how we can ***come-up-against*** pop culture's caricature and boldly and wildly snatch our kids back from the fatal attraction of its funhouse mirror. To begin, we would like for you to take a quick test to calculate the differences between two word banks. We are going to state some words and we want you to look at each word carefully. This is a test of your ability to find relationships among groups of words—we're teachers right? See if you can identify the main commonality when all of the words are placed together as a whole. Ready? Word-set #1--

overhead, dittoes, chalkboard, paper, pencil, ruler,
notebook, backpack, tests, scantron, markers, tape,
desks, crayons, calculator, glue, textbooks, eraser,
pencil sharpener, hall pass, pens, tacks, magnets,
dictionary, desks, tables, ***teachers, students***

Any ideas . . . ? Absolutely you do. We asked students to
identify the relationship among these data and all of the students
immediately came up with an identical answer. The answer is
<u>school</u>! Not a shocking revelation, is it? Consider the next set of
words and do the same analysis. Ready? Word set #2-

MTV, Soap Operas, Rap, Hip-Hop, Video Games,
Make Up, Goth, Tatoos, Body Piercing, Smoking,
40 Ounces, BET, Drugs, Gambling, Pre-Marital Sex,
Fast Food, Cars, American Idol, Happy Meals,
Fear Factor, Television (Dora the Explorer, Sponge Bob),
I-pod, Mp3, Boom-Boxes, Game Shows, Coffee Shops,
Bongs, Harry Potter, ***Many Student, No Teachers***

When you look at this set of words, what relationships
do you see among these data? When we asked students what
relationship they saw within this word bank . . . they ALL stated,
"FUN". ***Hopefully, you realized that many of these pop culture
icons have endless potential for frightening-fun, but so much so
that they are euthanizing our youth.*** Notice the vast difference
betweeen the two sets of word banks. If you were a student, which
word bank would you see as more intriguing and inviting? No
brainer! Introducing the polar entities called "School Smart"
and "Street Smart". Guess which word bank is "Street Smart"?
Duh! We proclaim that the huge gap between the two "smarts"
is the festering etiology driving the achievement gap. The human
condition that is inherent in both youth and pop culture is rarely
given air-time within the context of schooling. The monumental
dicotomy between pencils and erasers and body piercing and

bongs is as far as the East is from the West!

The second set of words are highly inflamable and a classroom discussion/discourse around any one of them must be done with consternation, developmental and age-appropriateness, and with great care. We are not at all advocating that a teacher lights-up-a-joint while standing next to the overhead to relate to the students; rather we firmly believe that *teaching void of full comprehension of pop culture's influence and the human condition is like pouring honey all over ourselves while bear hunting!* How can we, as teachers, utilize pop culture as an informative tool to Reach Em' to Teach Em'? IF "It Takes a Whole Village to Prepare a Teacher" (which we firmly believe that it does), how can we integrate pop culture in meaningful, ethical, and developmentally-appropriate ways? We believe that these two polar entities can be superimposed by using great wisdom and artful pedagogy. We have presented our research at many conferences; in particular at the Pop Culture Association/American Culture Association's National and Regional Conferences for several years. We are thrilled to bring our research data to you in a more condensed format.

To begin to answer the question of "how", we need to quickly turn to the research by C.M. Charles, author of *The Synergetic Classroom: Joyful Teaching and Gentle Discipline.* His upbeat text identifies how future teachers can create a classroom environment than enlivens instruction (imagine that)! He states:

"Students quickly disengage from tasks they find boring, meaningless, or frustrating. They then look for something more interesting to do, such as daydreaming or talking and joking with others".

Dr. Charles asked students why they mishave and eventually engage is very, very troublesome behavior. The students candidly stated two very profound utterances.

#1 "WE ARE BORED" #2 "WE JUST WANNA HAVE FUN!"

Fellow Chalksters . . . don't you find these responses rather unimpressive? And, in some ways, doesn't it tick-you-off? The real reality (moron-oxy!) is that what appears to be their rather mundane mentality may hold great enlightment for us. HARK . . . there are many hidden pearls within our hard-shelled school oysters! Let's get out the crab-crackers and see what can be exposed!

Students were quick to state that they were "bored" in school . . . Yeah, yeah, yeah and your point is? Our point is not a shocking revelation; it's one that is very predictable. To be brutally honest, students feel that magnetic-pull between the **ho-hum** "school-smart" and the **seductive** "street-smart" polar entities.

All one has to do is gain entrance into the weird and wild mind of the students to realize that they define "boredom"as school! Remember educators... Teachers are from Mars-- Students are from Snickers!

Next . . . our precious students replied that the choice to misbehave is in direct correlation to the amount of "fun" that they are or are not having! Teachers, the equation looks something like this . . .

School + Havin' No Fun = Being a Pain in the Class!

How bout' that math teachers for a correctly-solved equation? Students were then asked to elaborate on the term "fun". In other words, they were invited to offer words to describe what "fun" really means to them. Without hesitation they offered 3 pedagogical pearls; ones that have the potential to change our instructional intent. When asked what the words boredom-in-school meant, they replied:

MOVE   TALK   LAUGH

Teachers, hear us now . . . this are some real pearls of wisdom that
have been extracted from the *raw oysters* themselves. Do you
realize what an incrediable revelation this is for us? Honestly,
these three words, move—talk—laugh are the very same words
that are aligned to pop culture.

Now, let's revisit the two word banks. Ask yourself,
"Which word bank is all-about moving, talking, and laughing"?
Well . . . that would be word bank #2!!!!! Pop culture's allurement
is all about the movement of the body and movement of the mouth!
Media today, within our villages, effectively sells the concepts of
move, talk, and laugh. *Schools today* fail to sell the concepts of sit
quietly, don't talk, be still, take your seat, stop laughing. Remember
Charlie Brown' teacher---Blah, Blah Blah, Blah! After all, the
school culture advocates that "fun" is a separate entity and should
be saved for recess and lunch.   What is it that we teachers don't
get about this whole thing? After all, how many of us have (year
after year) attended boring professional development workshops
in which we are not free to move, talk and laugh? We sat there the
entire day thinking . . . B-O-R-I-N-G! Simplistically speaking,
the body has a unique design and has been crafted to move and
talk! If a body sets for long, long periods of time and not used, it
will atrophy. If a mind is untouched and left to gather moth and
dust, it will surely become bored, waste away, and eventually die.
We are beings-of-movement complete with specialized modes of
communication.

With this in mind, we are stressing the importance of
teachers making a valiant effort to get-to-know the village that
they teach within. Why? We have to understand the stuff going-
on-in-the-village to clearly make sense of our competition and
expose the predators that lurk about and prey on our youth. When
we have a full comprehension of the village, we can better discern
our educational enemies and the reasons why students are falling
victim to pop culture's negative influence. We *guarantee* that the
thoughts that our students are thinking are greatly influenced by
what goes on OUTSIDE the classroom. We *guarantee* that the
thoughts teachers are thinking are greatly influenced by what goes

on OUTSIDE the classroom! (The fruit doesn't fall far from the fruitcake!)

Knowing these outside influences allows us to transform the forces of evil that try desperately to slam-dunk our kids and destroy their self-image, self-worth, and potential to capture their purpose. (Check out the next chapter about how Superhero teachers are fighting against these forces!) Lastly, we want to clarify that we are, in no way, suggesting that *everything* within our modern village is negatively affecting our kids. There are many forces and institutions that are trying to lift our children up. These dynamic outside influences are ones that we must identify, embrace, and tap-into. The following are bullet point suggestions as starting points to assist you in gathering important data about your village. These bullet points will help you frame your instruction and assessment aligned to those exciting, innovative, and captivating standards and benchmarks! Think about how each one of these words can be utilized as instructional tools. In fact, Consider some "F" words and instructional examples of how you can integrate pop culture within a lesson along with ways to combat the "mean and nasties" inherent in many pop culture icons.

- Food—Where are your students eating outside of the home front? Are they eating at Taco Bell (a.k.a. Taco Smell), McDonalds, KFC, Burger King, etc.? Is there a local coffee shop or greasy spoon that they go for breakfast or to buy a Coney Dog, Pepsi and fries? Have you ever considered using menus, store posters, nutritional charts, children's meals with toys (there are very interesting figures on the kid's meals ripe for discussion and analysis) and other various signs/marketing flyers from some of these fast-food places? These generate great excitement within students and can be used as instructional tools and a catalyst for motivation. They can be hung up in the classroom much like a poster. When students come into the classroom and see something very familiar from their village they ALWAYS comment and get-geaked!

Menus from a local restaurant are pop culture artifacts and can be utilized across many subjects and concepts. You can use a menu to discover affordability . . . for example, *"Susie was hanging out at Burger King for lunch. She had exactly $5.45 in her Louis Vuitton knock-off purse that she bought on the streets of New York! Name three combinations of food from this menu that she can afford to buy!"* Or . . . *"Students, I am handing out a Mickey-Dees nutritional chart that Ronald McDonald gave me while I was cruising around the drive thru. Man, that dude has some serious red hair! Calculate the percentage of carbohydrates, sugar, salt, and protein in one McDonald's double cheeseburger. Remember, we are beginning our unit on 'America the Buffet!'—cool huh?"* We find the managers in these establishments very willing to accommodate and give us any item we need from a life size standing poster of Darth Vader to 25 Happy Meal boxes with toys! Again, these are the items that serve as décor for the classroom. Sorry, the problem–solving chart and process writing chart from a teacher's store is not a major turn-on for kids! How many of you have children who ask for a gift certificate from the teacher's store for their birthday? Using these fast food icons, students can look for nouns, verbs and phrases to support a grammar lesson or draw inferences regarding stereotypes, gender issues, or geographical areas for social studies and to determine good and poor nutritional choices for health class. The students will think it is totally cool that they are seeing an actual menu/poster from one of their favorite hang outs instead of a ditto or chart from the teacher's store (boring)! There are many, many ways to use artifacts from restaurants. Our favorite is to bring in large KFC Buckets for a language arts lesson. Why not place a rubber chicken in the bucket and set it on a desk at the front of the classroom. Why not design a dynamic rubric, aligned to the standards, and ask the students to write a two-page story "From the chicken's point-of-view". By the way, students love this one—it's a crack up or should we say--a real cluck up! Try it and if you are lucky, the KFC manager might throw in some Original Recipe samples!! Thanks Colonel Sanders—love those chicken wings, but know that they are full of fat, salt, and calories. Finger lickin' good!

Food can be one of those evil forces in the village in that fast food is very detrimental to our children and society as a whole. Our youth continue to make poor nutritional choices and will still select fries over apples most of the time. Fast food is part of pop culture. Teachers can use fast food choices as a way to expose poor nutritional content and empty foods (salt, sugar, and fat) that are correlated to disease. Rich dialogue can emerge about how these joints market their meals and how advertising targets youth. Clearly, many of our girls struggle with anorexia and bulimia and suffer greatly from this disease that generates empty promises. We can't tell you how many times we have confronted this head-on using pop culture items from fast food establishments.

- Finances/Fashion/Fun—What are students spending their money on? What do they like to do for fun? What are they wearing? Are they using their own money (or their parent's finances) to purchase toys, CD's, I-pods, Nike tennis shoes, MP3's, *Cosmopolitan* or *US Magazine*, cars, sports equipment, make-up, drugs, guns, alcohol, bongs, designer clothing and other pop culture items? In fact, it's under this section that we consistently find students purchasing items correlated to their self-image and self-worth. They will also purchase things that will seemingly help-them-fit-in to the peer group/gang of their choice. Determining what's hot and what's not for our students will better inform us as to what they highly value and how it is much more relevant and exciting than our dittoes, texts, outlines, films, etc. Are there sneaky ways to use these items as instructional tools? The answer is a resounding

YEP! Consider the typical middle-school girl who wants to look like a Diva! It seems like the ***designing-divas-syndrome*** begins as early as first grade and never ends for some (even in college)! So . . . she shops at all the cool stores, buys expensive make up at the mall, and has to have her hair done just-so at the salon-spa. Her shirt has to be tight and revealing, her shoes pointed and high, and earrings dangling and long. Does this sound familiar? She measures her value by how many guys show her attention and attempt to fondle her. How tragic. Time for school uniforms! Anyway, how can teachers prey on this kind of pop culture? We would begin by sending a letter home to the parent/guardian(s) informing them that we will be using magazines targeting our young girls. We would list the magazines and reveal to them that we will be creating a case study about a young woman who felt driven to fit-in and would stop at nothing to be loved. This scenario would speak to the issue of the perception of beauty and acceptance. The purpose of this inquiry lesson will be to engender discourse about how young women are targeted by various companies. We will identify specific strategies used by companies to market their theme entitled, "Sex Sells". At the end of the lesson, students (especially young women) will have opportunities, bi-weekly, to meet and discuss the pitfalls of media under the direction of a mature female teacher. Following this lesson, we would move to the socially-constructed concept of, "What does it mean to be a male?" Again, we would pull magazines and movies that depict a ***real-male*** as one with strong—sexy abs, a 6 pack on his stomach, and one that resembles a physique like Superman or Hercules. Think of the possibilities... The end result is a classroom mural to be painted in the community by the students that demystifies stereotypes and sexuality. There are certainly many other potential "end results" that a teacher can craft.

Fashion is something that is an integral part of a student's perceived power. We have traveled around to many, many stores in various malls (Claire's, Limited Too, Gap, Nike, Express, Guess, etc) and each have been very willing to give us store posters, coupons, and signs that we can utilize for the purpose of curriculum alignment. We have been in many classrooms and have modeled to teachers how to integrate fashion into their instruction. For example, Nike stores are very excited to give teachers shoe boxes. How would you utilize a shoe box that has the logo "Air Jordan" on the outside? Regarding math, students can identify various shapes that the box can engender. For younger children, teachers can have children sort various shapes that they have placed in the box or use it as an estimating box filled with various items. Measurement is a concept that can be taught using this pop culture artifact. To enhance English concepts, the box can be filled with 3x5 cards labeled with many words and the students can work in pairs to create a sentence. They can also separate the nouns, verbs, adjectives and place in different boxes. We have modeled many cross-disciplinary lessons that transform shoe boxes as "center boxes". One center box can be constructed to teach-to the concept of "electricity". Within the box the student will find an instruction sheet with inquiry-driven questions along with materials needed to correctly construct a model to successfully conduct electricity. The end result is that the light bulb must illuminate. Center boxes can be used in the classroom or taken home to wok in collaboration with the parent. Students identify with the logos, stores, and their artifacts.

- Friends—Who are our students hangin' out with? Peer groups and peer pressure groups are very much driven by the influence of pop. Friends are the thermometer upon which our students measure their hotness or coldness with regard to relationships (male and female). Their self worth and image are calculated daily by friends and the old funhouse mirror that reflects what their friends desire in them—not what they know to be true about themselves. Again, how tragic. There are large groups of students who have no friends and that is devastating and severely lonely. Those without friends usually fall victim to measuring themselves by pop culture's "Loser Scale"! Friends are living, breathing, and rather intimidating pop icons! Sometimes friends can be dynamic powersources and pain relievers. We have, just like you, seen both extremes! As a teacher, we again would hit this "F" word head on and examine popular living icons that are seen as idols by our students. We would bring in posters of their favorite idols and dialogue about the differences between an idol and role model. We would ask them if they would rather have an idol for a friend or a role model and why? Our goal would be to eventually remove the posters of those whom they said were their idols and replace them with large pictures of their grandfather, a rabbi, their mom, or maybe their coach. You see, the carnage of pop culture would certainly reveal idols to be worshipped by our youth. Let's replace these idols with mentors whose footprints provide a pathway, not to success, but to stewardship.

- Family— Understanding the dynamics of the family is critical in reaching and teaching. Understanding the vast diversity within each family is even more powerful. Do you know who clearly recognizes the needs, stressors and diversity of the family? THE MEDIA! Media influences prey upon the vulnerabilities of both the family as a struggling unit as well as the individual members who are trying to set themselves apart. Our families are constantly struggling to define and identify themselves against some standard of measurement. What standard do you measure your family unit by? Interesting question, isn't it? Television has showered our living rooms with many examples and standards for families. Lets list some (past to present): Sky King, The Flintstones, Father Knows Best, The Jetsons, Leave It To Beaver, All in the Family, The Nanny, The Partridge Family, The Jeffersons, Cosby Show, Happy Days, Bewitched, Brady Bunch, Eight Is Enough, Family Ties, Family Affair, Family Matters, The Brady Bunch, The Simpsons, The Beverly Hillbillies, Growing Pains, My Three Sons, The Munsters, The Adams Family, The Walton's, My Two Dads, The Osbornes, Home Improvement, Family Guy, Rugrats, Sponge-Bob, Everyone Loves Raymond, and That Seventies Show (to name only a few)! Do you recall some of those oldies? Pop culture is ever present in the living rooms, bedroom, kitchens and even the garages of many families. Again, we are not stating that everything that television has brought into our homes is horrible; no way! To see the vast diversity within many of these television shows has been great instruments for increased self-worth and self-image. The teacher must first become keenly aware of what is going on within the families of those children they serve. Certainly, this is NOT for the purpose of intrusion, but to identify how they can better serve their children. What goes on at home goes on in the heart and head of the student. Family vulnerabilities (disease, death, illness, divorce, poverty, separation, adoption, foster care, incarceration) are forces that spill over and flood into the classroom. To ignore these, lessens our ability to reach students and families. To teach within the context of family, diversity, and the human condition of the family, is part of our exciting work as educators. Family television shows are fabulous pop culture icons for teachers to deconstruct and study the power of difference and similarity. While many of pop's media influences go against the health and well-being of the diverse family, teachers can use these as springboards to confront the many "isms" inherent within these productions. Teachers can also build upon concepts by utilizing the popularity of shows. For example, an elementary teacher might set up 3 learning centers that reflect three popular children's television shows including Rugrats, Sponge-Bob, and Dora the Explorer. At each center, the teacher has gathered various artifacts that reflect each show. Using a rubric at each center, the students can move throughout the room and compare and contrast such concepts as: main character, plot, setting, family make–up, protagonist, antagonist, etc. Pop culture, in particular, their construction of the family unit, is a powerful entity for teachers to prey upon as well as embrace.

There are many ways to take everyday objects/pop culture artifacts) and turn them into an exciting and useful teaching/assessment tools in the classroom. Consider a pizza box (fractions), pickle jar (circumference), hanger (triangle), toilet seat or hula hoops--student's favorite of all time (Venn Diagram), potato chip bag (depth), curling iron (circuit), milk jug (volume), egg crate (storage) , jump ropes (graphic organizer), basket of diverse shoes (from the shoes' point of view), and macaroni (to use as commas on essays). What other ways might you juxtapose these items to your instruction? Our **Reach Em' To Teach Em'** workshops consist of 4 long tables full of what we call "village teaching supplies". To some, it may look like we are wild, hurry-up-and-retire-saleswomen from a thrift store. We virtually have our teaching nuggets spread out all over the room. We even have several tables full of costumes, masks, silly hats and glasses and wild accessories. We value these tools because it ignites our students unlike any item that we have ever found at a teacher's store. Colleagues, "returning to the lost art of simplistic teaching' means that we use the village as the primary instruction tools and lessons. Remember, "It Takes A Whole Village To Prepare A Teacher"! Simple teaching is what joy-engendering is all about. Teaching and fun are meant to be synonymous. Remember, fun means move, talk and laugh!

We are bummed to report that there are actually some

teachers and administrators that believe that when it comes to learning, there is no room for fun and that play is left to pre-schoolers. There are those who advocate that teaching is not a performance art—BOOOO HISSS! We whole heartedly disagree. A considerable amount of learning takes place in the formative pre-school years during play as well as the formative older years during play (in which we have substituted the term play for recreation to make it sound mature). Play is performance and performance is play! The act of playing/recreating is an important tool that influences any life. The primary goals of childhood as well as "older and in the hood" are to grow, learn, and play. It is often through play that children learn to make sense of the world around them. A child not only is invited to learn content, but is also absorbing social skills toward increasing self-image and self-worth. Who says that playing and learning together has to stop after kindergarten (must be Scrooge)! We firmly believe that play and learning dance the two-step. For many of our children, play infers watching television for hours and hours on-end! Why not use their knowledge of television programming to our advantage and as a teaching tool. Then eventually, we can combat television with more healthy choices at home, like engaging in dynamic learning tasks driven by a contagious rubric.

For example, ***The Price is Right*** is a game show that, for some crazy reason, attracts our youth. It must be the "Bob Barker" appeal that lures them in. Game shows are a dynamic way to support information that students need for a firm conceptual foundation. Imitating the format of this T.V. wonder can not only help students apply math, but it allows a teacher to assess whether he/she needs to reteach concepts. After all, why would teachers set their students up for failure? In other words, why would you administer a teacher-made test if you are not absolutely sure that they are at mastery? It also gives a teacher insight into whether or not the students are ready for the next set of data in the lesson. Remember, teaching and checking for comprehension go hand and hand. Below you will see a sample of other ideas we pulled from a very long list of Reach Em' to Teach Em' tools. If you use any of these in your classroom, BRAVO!! If you see something new, we challenge you to try them. Some of these ideas are from other teachers and some we came up with on our own. We must admit that we could speak about teaching 24-8! Teachers who share ideas with one another should be applauded. After all, it is about the students, and not about us.

Go ahead; go outside your comfort zone, perform pedagogical mutiny...we dare ya!

Pointers

Pointers seem to be a valuable and a joy-igniting tool in the classroom. Sure, the infamous yard stick, laser pointer works, but it can also seem boring and non-stimulating. No matter what age level you teach, goofy pointers add ***pizzazz*** to any lecture or lesson. As a matter of fact, some students love creating pointers for the classroom. We have seen many classrooms that include an umbrella bucket filled with pointers. Many of which were made by students themselves. Some of our pointers include a toilet plunger, manikin foot on a stick or hand on a stick, tree branch, a dowel with a stuffed glove attached to it, golf club, mop and many more. Pointer possibilities are endless!

Games

Students love to learn content from games show simulations. (Remember the Price is Right example?) Media sells!! Game shows test our cognitive regurgitation reflex! How about this idea...have your students create a giant game on a plain white shower curtain liner. These giant games help aide in learning content at all levels of any taxonomy. We also love using the game ***Twister*** to help students practice content. For example, math; if a student spins and lands on a blue dot, he/she must reduce the fraction correctly in order to remain on that dot. Of course you can use any type of content with a ***Twister*** mat. We found our ***Twister*** game at a thrift store for 50 cents. Whoa, what a deal—won't find that price at the teacher's store!

Balls

Pre-made content balls can be purchased at some teacher's stores and in some catalogues, but they can be pretty pricey and they may or may not have the exact content you are looking for. So why don't you make your own? We find beach balls of all sizes at dollar stores and write content on them with permanent marker...waa-laa! It's an inexpensive way to create content balls with just the right content. You can divide the ball up into various sections and write things like nouns, verbs, adjectives, etc. The ball is thrown around to students and when one catches it, whatever their right thumb lands upon, they have to give an example of that part of speech. Students love these learning spheres and they work across curriculum. Go ahead have a ball! (ok . . . that was lame)

Overhead Makeover

It is no secret that overhead projectors lack personality and are about as exciting as a yardstick pointer. First graders, because it is new to them, may be the only grade that doesn't groan at the thought of a teacher using an overhead. To students, an overhead equals taking notes. Taking notes equals tests. Tests equal school. Note-taking is not a popular task but certainly one that is critical. Finding a way to diffuse the boring properties of an overhead is not an easy task either, but we took the challenge. We went back to one of our favorite movies, *"**The Brave Little Toaster"**. The story line is not important to my point here, but the characters are. In this movie, inanimate objects such as appliances are personified into great characters. We decided to play off of that concept by dressing up an overhead to simulate the same idea. We add google eyes and a wig or hat to help give the overhead an identity. The students love to name the overhead, and over time, it becomes a part of the classroom community. While we are lecturing, at certain times, we stop and have a conversation with our new buddy! High school students think that this is such a hoot!

Puppets

Okay, that's enough. I know what some of you are thinking! Some of you are cringing at the whole idea of using puppets. Not an uncommon occurrence until…you really get to explore that wonderful concept of puppet pedagogy. The fact is puppets have been around for over 2,000 years. They've been entertaining and teaching for a very long time. Look at the brilliance of the late Jim Henson. His master mind in the world of edutainment using "The Muppets" took learning to a new level. "Sesame Street" is proof of how puppets can influence the lives of children and adults alike. We take our bags of over 100 puppets (many that are 3 feet in height) into classrooms around the United States and have not been disappointed by the results. Children and adults have found themselves immersed in the character they hold on their hand and experience the joy of puppets. They can be used across curriculum and do not have to be an expensive investment if resources don't allow. We have taken our graduate classes to thrift stores and asked them to put on their creativity hats and use anything with in the store to create a puppet. We gave them a specific rubric and away they went. It was a fun joyful and thought-provoking experience. Students claimed that the experience took them to a different level in that they had to really spend time thinking about whom they were and who they were not. The finished product left us in tears and on the floor laughing.

We understand that not everyone will adhere to these different strategies presented. We do believe, however, that shifting in and out of different paradigms can be beneficial in increasing JOY in the classroom for both student and teacher. Face it, times are changing! We live in a fast food world where diverse stimuli are at an all time high. These stimuli can be both unpredictable and catastrophic to what we are trying to accomplish in the classroom. With the barriers (stimuli) that block our messages to our students, we need to beat pop culture at its own game. Part of this paradigm shift includes nurturing a classroom family where each person in the class respects and knows the interests and strengths of each individual. A community is built upon the idea that the students and teacher are there to help one another in all aspects of the learning process. For some teachers, building a solid classroom community IS a paradigm shift. According to C.M. Charles (the gentlemen we previously referenced), Emeritus Faculty at San Diego State University and leader in classroom management, states that there are nine elements needed for synergy in the classroom. Using these elements below, a teacher can begin/further their paradigm transformation from one that is teacher-centered to one that is community-centered. They are as follows:

- Ethics
- Trust
- Charisma
- Communication
- Interest
- Class agreement
- Cooperation
- Human relations
- Problem resolution

Utilizing all of these elements can bring forth a dynamic energy within a classroom. While our workshops play-off of all of these attributes of a dynamic classroom, let us focus for a minute on the element named "Interest". Charles declares that, "The learning activities to which you invite students must be made interesting enough to attract and hold their involvement. You will learn how to organize activities so that they intrigue students and satisfy their needs". Most students hold teachers as THE most important adults within their lives. Therefore, it is important we are always aware of what messages, verbal and nonverbal, we bring forth.

Delivering content can be a difficult task. Students verbalize boredom with virtually everything EXCEPT pop culture! How can that be? Boredom is the prescription for creating monsters! Again, remember that students want to move, talk, and laugh (fun-fulfillers). Teachers naturally try to suppress these human acts out of fear of losing control of the classroom. I guess the next question is what kind of control are you trying to have? The key is not for the teacher to control the classroom, but for the teacher to teach the students to control themselves. Internal accountability needs to take place.

Let's admit the obvious! We don't hear too many students these days saying that they love school. How many of us confirm their dislikes about school and say, "Yeahhhh, school is just something you have to do. Deal with it and get over your pity party!" Clearly, standards are dictating a lot of our curriculum, but how we align to these mandates IS where instruction should meet the human condition. Furthermore, we want our students talking about us. We believe that if our students aren't talking about us, then are we really doing our job? We want them to talk intensively about our pedagogy! We want to create an atmosphere where the gossip in the school is about the wild, crazy or innovative stuff going on. If teachers take the time to know what their students are interested in (pop culture), what the students needs are (self-image and self-worth), and what gets the students excited (stuff that makes them move, talk, and laugh) our classroom joy will move in a northern direction, while boredom heads south for the winter!

We hear our colleagues continually say that time doesn't allow for integration of many creative things. We acknowledge the time restrictions that school seems to be all about! Yet, time is a constant but our methods do not have to be! We both can speak of the endless hours we spend creating/crafting/recreating/retooling seemingly boring curriculum and instruction. For example, creating a time machine out of a box and gathering costumes to role play a fictitious character named "Professor Bedrock", is critical to igniting joy and increasing student comprehension within a simple geography lesson. There is no room for laziness in teaching. If you do not consider yourself a "creative" person, seek out or team up with a colleague that is an out-of-the-boxer teacher! Ask her/him to help you spice up a lesson. We, as chalk-maestros, need to come together for the common good of the students.

There are so many people that believe that great institutions breed great teachers. We believe that it isn't the institution that breeds the greatness, it is the character and calling that IS the institution of greatness. Character is an institution! The development of character has to come from the depths of one's soul. This maturity is bred and fashioned within the precious walls that encase "The Place of Further Still". It is the realness of the heartfelt—the unwavering, unconditional love that enlists one into combat on the pedagogical battlefield. Unceasing love musters-up contagious passion. Unyielding commitment to authentic (simplistic) learning is the impetus for creating and recreating the possibilities of each mind. We, as **servants to the children and chalk**, have an incredible responsibility that cannot be taken lightly. Master-informers know this and live by it. They thrive and rely on it. It is a responsibility that is taken to such a degree that there is no room for selfishness or sell-out-ness. ATTENTION EDUCATORS: NO COMPROMISE ALLOWED ON SCHOOL PROPERTY! Teachers' narratives can make or break the spirit of our students. It is important that we take an inventory of our own fiber and self-efficacy to make sure that we are affecting our students in the positive way that they so richly deserve. Character DOES count and the mechanism for obtaining it, many times, is the great pain that we endure and persevere. This is the foundation upon which those **sold-out-to-the-children** are grown and manicured.

Being a teacher is not just a job, a joke, a choice, a career, or a profession. It is an investment into the lives of children. It is an answer to a chalk-summons. If we are only about the math, social studies, sciences, and English, and less about the human condition of the child and family, we will lose the very essence of our call. Teaching and learning should transcend throughout one's entire life. Teachers are called to work in the intersection where pedagogy kisses the human condition. . . . .

Chapter 5
"Raising a Super Child in a Not So Super World"

"Once upon a time there was a teacher. She was an ordinary teacher that by a simple glance seemed nothing too special. She wore nothing special and her hair was 'just so'. She was quiet and held a sweet demeanor that seemed to attract the likes of many students within the school. I even felt drawn to her as she gently floated down the hall with confidence and quiet humility. From time to time I would walk to the window of my classroom just to watch her in the hall hoping to find an answer to her mystery. She was not like the rest of us. No one really disliked her, and they couldn't figure out why they liked her. She did not engage in our mindless, verbal student-bashing that we did in the teacher's lounge or publicly air the frustrations of school bureaucracy. No one could simply figure her out and couldn't verbalize why they didn't like her. Other teachers were jealous of her but couldn't pin-point exactly why. She was our mystery teacher for sure! At times this teacher would say things that were so weird and always perplexing. I found myself running away from her when I saw her coming toward me; it's easier not to have any interactions with her. Yet, sometimes I got caught! For example, we were both in the teacher's lounge grabbing a cup of coffee and the silence was uncomfortable. I decided to simply ask her what she does in her classroom to stop discipline problems. She immediately looked directly at me with her big, brown eyes, smiled and said, "I think of discipline as a process of training children to initiate self-control; to develop internal accountability which will lead to self-worth." I stared at her with much confusion and said, "Huh?" She again smiled and told me how much she enjoyed working in the building with so many wonderful professionals. I smiled back and told her thank you. Clearly she had not been in *my* class! And, I'm not convinced that our mystery teacher *really* has a handle on our kids and the neighborhoods they come from! Regardless, I did hash and rehash her words for two weeks trying to figure out what she meant.

About two months into the school year, I realized that I had the class from hell! This, by far, was the hardest group of kids I have ever had. It is only November, and I have no connection with my students at all. I was having a worse than normal day and I was about to lose it. I dropped off my students at their gym class and sat down in the lounge. Well, guess who walked in while I was there—yes, you guessed it, the mystery teacher. She was the last person that I wanted to see at this time. She sat down next to me, big brown eyes looking right at me. I told her that I was upset because I wasn't connecting with my students at all—the truth be known, they could give-a-flip! I asked her if she had any suggestions for me. Well, she sent me another zinger that hit me straight between the eyes. "Are you familiar with belle hooks, a famous African-American educator? Isn't it interesting to know that she uses lower case letters to spell her full name—I am quite intrigued by this" she stated. I told her that I was familiar with that 'hooks-lady' because she spoke at a local university last year and I was unable to go and that I was glad because I heard she was boring. She told me that belle hooks believes that when a teacher enters the classroom, she enters it with the conviction and that it was crucial that both teacher and student are active participants, not a passive consumers. And, that education would surely connect the will to know with the will to become!" I stared at her for a long time and thought, "Huh?" (POW, ZAP, ZING, ZOWIE!!!) Well, she did it again. I smiled, thanked her, and walked out to the parking lot.

Well, the drive home was awful! My head hurt as I tried to figure out the strange message that was etched in my brain from our mystery teacher. My feet hurt from the day and my frustration level seemed to only increase at the thought of walking into a house full of yet another bunch of out-of-control kids! I took a deep breath as I walked into a toy-infested house. The first thing I did was trip on a stack of my youngest son's superhero books. I almost started yelling in a rage of fury when a little bell rang in my head. I scurried to my feet, grabbed his books, kissed the kids on their heads and ran to my office and shut the door. Breathing hard, I grabbed a yellow pad and a pen. This is it! I think that I might have solved the dilemma of this mystery teacher across the hall.

I read silently, with excitement, from my son's **Superhero Encyclopedia**, a book that he just had to have for his birthday. At that time, I thought, "What a waste of thirty-dollars!" This book outlined many things about a superhero including their attributes. As I carefully read, not missing a word, I observed rather weird statements that for some reason began to make sense to me. I sat there for several hours reading and taking notes on a book that once had the potential to be tossed in the trash! As I continued to take notes, I came upon the definition of the term "superhero". It read, "A superhero is a heroic character with a selfless, prosocial mission; who possesses superpowers, advanced technology, mystical abilities, or highly developed physical and or mental skills; who has a super identity and iconic costume." (POW, ZAP, ZING, ZOWIE!) The word 'huh' in my brain turned into a big, fat 'YEAH'!

Immediately, I thought of our little mystery teacher. Thoughts were swilling in my brain. I thought to myself, "Naw ... she couldn't be a ... super hero, could she?" I began getting rather paranoid! I felt like the back-end of a donkey! I immediately reflected upon every conversation we had and looking back on everything I saw her do. Wow! She is definitely selfless; I have never heard anything coming from her that is hurtful or self-serving. She is always on a mission for her students and her superpowers are the ways she seems to connect with her students. Her mystical abilities are just that; mystical! She seems to possess a power over people without showing any power. She is also very humble. Interesting! And, she wears ugly, black glasses much like Clark Kent, a.k.a. Superman!

By this time, I really started freaking out! I grabbed a Diet Pepsi and continued my search! I looked at the attributes and decided to take the next several months observing her and her students to see if there were correlations. I decided not to tell anyone. Setting up an experiment to look for superhero attributes in a fellow teacher would certainly win me a quick trip to the Tenure Board Hearings or the state mental hospital! On my yellow pad of paper, I listed out the attributes leaving room to take notes as I went along in my journey. I decided to secretly get my students involved by asking them to observe another class of students and write out all of the positive things they hear and see. We decided to observe the mystery teacher's class (wonder how that happened). I molded this assignment into a "character counts" lesson and aligned it to the standard on teaching "Core Democratic Values". Our classroom now seemed to begin to take a rather different turn on learning.

Together, we recorded data from our observations. For once, we both became active participants. I thought to myself, "Huh!" I had remembered what our mystery teacher said about that 'belle hooks' researcher. Did I really now have both the "will to know and the will to become"? This whole thing was getting really rather bizarre! My entire classroom dynamics had gone from frustration to fantastic. Believe it or not, after school I ran home, grabbed my kids, ran them through McDonald's, got them a hamburger (what else would I get!) and went to the movie to see . . . "The Fantastic Four"—a superhero movie! On the way, I stopped by the bookstore to by belle's books.

The next day, I asked my students to turn in their observations and write ups. Rather than me lecturing on 'Core Democratic Values' or giving them a worksheet, we had a debate. I dressed up as Judge Judy and I used a toilet plunger for a gavel. For once they were really excited and I had zero discipline problems. Can you even believe they wanted to design another assignment and create their own individual superhero! I thought to myself, "Huh?" I couldn't believe that they were taking reasonability and initiating more work. Could that be the 'internal accountability' that Miss Mystery Teacher was speaking of?

That evening I couldn't wait to get home. I went immediately into my office and looked over the data that the students had collected. After reading through these data, it became very clear to me why this teacher not only had a positive impact on her students, but on me as well. I took their data and aligned it under each of the superhero attributes. Here is what I found:

- ## Attribute #1 *Secret Identity*
  Her humble existence secretly, yet openly, exploited and modeled good moral character generally without a lot of words. She is a hope-giver with obvious unconditional love for her students. They feel very safe in her classroom.

- ## Attribute #2 *Superhuman Powers & Abilities*

  I always witness this teacher going the extra mile for her students. She had no problem admitting when she was wrong. She modeled strength as well as vulnerabilities. She showed tough love when needed, holding her students in a state of grace. She practices the poem by Dorothy Law Nolte that states . . .

  If a child lives with criticism, he learns to condemn
  If a child lives with hostility, he learns to fight
  If a child lives with ridicule, he learns to be shy
  If a child lives with shame, he learns to feel guilty
  If a child lives with tolerance, he learns to be patient
  If a child lives with encouragement, he learns confidence
  If a child lives with praise, he learns to appreciate
  If a child lives with fairness, he learns justice
  If a child lives with security, he learns to have faith
  If a child lives with approval, he learns to like himself
  If a child lives with acceptance and friendship, he learns to find love in the world.

Our mystery teacher models life-giving techniques, not life-taking techniques. This also sounds like a lesson teaching 'Core Democratic Values'!

- Attribute #3 ***Master of Relevant Skills/ Equipment***

It was amazing to me how she is able to tune herself into the different learning styles and differences within her students. She takes a student's greatest weakness and makes it their greatest strength! She has incredible skills in knowing the diverse needs of each student. She molds her instruction to their individual needs. Instead of looking at all of the students the same, she embraces differences in gender, ethnicity, etc. She is clearly a great listener and knows how much can be learned when one listens more and speaks less. She models more than she speaks. She brings in parents and uses items in the community to help her reach her students. She even listens to the music that her students are captivated with. Her teaching tools and equipment is carefully and craftfully utilized in a very different manner in which it was intended. For example, she uses Hula Hoops to help students comprehend the concept of using a Venn diagram! Kids are rarely sitting in their desks.

- Attribute #4 ***Willing to Risk Life & Limb in Service of Good Without the Thought of Reward***

I will never forget this year's whole school holiday celebration in December. She was in charge of this (no one else wanted anything to do with it!) and really put a new meaning in the word 'Happy' Holidays! Joyful, elated parents and students graced our school's hallways as they carried with large envelopes of money and unwrapped toys to be donated to an international orphanage. I remember hearing two parents speak standing by the lunchroom corridor. They were commenting on all of the service learning projects that their teacher was doing and how wonderful it was to have the gifts and money earned by the students, themselves. They especially commented on the many times that her class had been held at the nursing home in town for the purpose of studying the concept of diverse communities and caring. The older adults within the home were an integral part of the class and, in fact, were instrumental in destroying the many myths of the aging process. Our mystery teacher certainly was no mystery to her parents, community, and students! One parent stated that she had heard the teacher say that the greatest gift was that of love. Her modeling was evident in her students as they moved throughout the school and community.

- Attribute #5 ***Strong Sense of Idealism***

Her passivity, humility, and kindness has led me to the conclusion that she believes in teaching as a vibrant calling—one who is summoned to stand on a much higher ground. She works so incredibility hard (and makes it look so easy). Her ideals, character, and ethical walk are seemingly perfect. Her piercing, yet precious brown eyes encourage rather than demean. She redirects misbehavior and maintains positive, interactive relationships with her students. She never forces external obedience and respect. She teaches to the heart of the child and building strong, moral character is always her foremost motive.

- Attribute #6 ***Arch Enemies***

Our mighty mystery teacher clearly sees what roadblocks present barriers to student success (and she clearly articulates what success means!). She clearly knows what forces she is not in competition with for the hearts and minds of her students. She can easily tell you what movies, video games, television shows, and other things that her kids are into. She makes mighty connections and uses pop culture as weapons against those who seek to destroy and entice her students. She also keeps a close eye on other potential distractions outside of the classroom and stays connected to them through daily journaling and emails.

- ## Attribute #8 Iconic *Costume*

  I have seen over the course of the years many costumes worn by our mystery maiden. She has appeared as Susan B. Anthony, Johnny Appleseed, Rosa Parks, Velveeteen Rabbit, and many, many more. She even has a large costume box in her room for role playing. I never really paid much attention to it and always thought, "Oh how cute, a costume box". It now makes sense to me. Every afternoon, after school, she opens up the back part of her classroom for students to come to her "Monster Beauty Shop" if they get their homework done in class. They can give each other makeovers to look like monsters! Costumes make her lessons come alive as well as the many hats and glasses. What a cool idea!

The experience that we had studying the mystery teacher and her students was a catalyst for the beginning of a new direction in my life. It opened my eyes to a new attitude toward the way I envisioned life and how I viewed my classroom. I have begun a journey to seek my true purpose, one she has clearly found. I know it will be an act of true contemplation. I have come to realize that in these extreme times, extreme teaching must take place if I want to reach and teach my students. It's imperative that I utilize the whole village in making connections between the school and the streets; two blatant realities within a student's life. If I want to build a super child in this not so super world, I must hold myself accountable and not be deterred. I am driven now to find my purpose, continue to respond to my call to teach, model and instill superhero attributes, and create a marvel community. Then I can sit back and watch my little superheroes grow and one day stand in amazement as they put on their cape and boots and mightily serve those who follow them.

The Beginning (not the End . . .)

Author, M.V. O'Shea, former Professor of Education at the University of Wisconsin boldly declares, "The child's first heroes are the people who perform the striking dramatic, physical exploits. Their admiration for the firemen, policemen, chauffeurs, baseball stars, can be used in the interests of courage, persistence, self control. As they grow older, we must enrich their acquaintance with admirable types in worthwhile biographies. At every stage, however, the strongest influence will be exerted by the living examples of friends, parents, and teachers." As educators, we need to empower kids so they can become heroes themselves one day. Being a superhero (powersource) in a student's life means to encourage children to seek knowledge through positive praise and inquiry. Too often teachers are quick to use red marks on papers to accentuate what they did wrong rather than stamps and stickers that also highlight the positive. Red ink is a self-esteem destroyer. Try another color other than stark red to offer praise and correction. How about purple?

We, as superhero teachers, should turn these mistakes into learning experiences. Allowing a student to self-evaluate builds self accountability and self-esteem. Remember, teaching is not, or should not be teacher centered, but student centered. The calling of a teacher is like no other!!! Like many teachers before us and many to come, we really hold a great responsibility to the future job holders of our world. It only takes one word, one experience, one teacher to make or break the spirit of the child. It could clearly impact how that child views teachers, people, or school. Wouldn't you like to partake in a child's life as a superhero instead of their arch enemy?

Our dream is to see an entire school take on the components of a "Marvel Community". To have all the teachers, administrators and parents wear super hero capes every day. Where teachers and parents come together, where teachers and administrators work together and where little superheroes are being fashioned. Are we really far from this possibility? Can we look beyond ourselves for the greater good of humanity? Many of us already do.

"Proud To Be a Teacher" (author unknown)

"Where are the heroes of today?" a radio talk show host thundered. He blames society's shortcomings on education. Too many people are looking for heroes in all the wrong places. Movie stars and rock musicians, athletes, and models aren't heroes; they're celebrities. Heroes abound in public schools, a fact that doesn't make the news. There is no precedent for the level of violence, drugs, broken homes, child abuse, and crime in today's America. Education didn't create these problems but deals with them every day.

You want heroes?

Consider Dave Sanders, the school teacher shot to death while trying to shield his students from two youths on a shooting rampage at Columbine High School in Littleton, Colorado. Sanders gave his life, along with 12 students, and other less heralded heroes survived the Colorado blood bath.

You want heroes? Jane Smith, a Fayetteville, NC teacher, was moved by the plight of one of her students, a boy dying for want of a kidney transplant. So this woman told the family of a 14 year old boy that she would give him one of her kidneys. And she did. When they subsequently appeared together hugging on the Today Show, even Katie Couric was near tears.

You want heroes? Doris Dillon dreamed all her life of being a teacher. She not only made it, she was one of those wondrous teachers who could bring the best out of every single child. One of her fellow teachers in San Jose, Calif. said, "She could teach a rock to read." Suddenly she was stricken with Lou Gehrig's disease, which is always fatal, usually within five years. She asked to stay on job—and did. When her voice was affected she communicated by computer. Did she go home? Absolutely not! She is running two elementary school libraries! When the disease was diagnosed, she wrote the staff and all the families that she had one last lesson to teach—that dying is part of living. Her colleagues named her Teacher of the Year.

You want heroes? Bob House, a teacher in Gay, Georgia, tried out for "Who Wants to Be A Millionaire". After he won the million dollars, a network film crew wanted to follow up to see how it had impacted his life. New car? New house? Instead, they found both Bob House and his wife still teaching. They explained that it was what they had always wanted to do with their lives and that would not change. The community was both stunned and gratified.

You want heroes? Last year the average school teacher spent $468 of their own money for student necessities—workbooks, pencils-supplies kids had to have but could not afford. That's a lot of money from the pockets of the most poorly paid teachers in the industrial world.

Schools don't teach values? The critics are dead wrong. Public education provides more Sunday school teachers than any other profession. The average teacher works more hours in nine months than the average 40-hour employee does in a year.

You want heroes? For millions of kids, the hug they get from a teacher is the only hug they will get that day because the nation is living through the worst parenting in history. An Argyle, Texas kindergarten teacher hugs her little 5 and 6 year-olds so much that both the boys and the girls run up and hug her when they see her in the hall, at the football games, or in the malls years later. A Michigan principal moved me to tears with the story of her attempt to rescue a badly abused little boy who doted on a stuffed animal on her desk—one that said "I love you!" He said he'd never been told that at home. This is a constant in today's society—two million unwanted, unloved, abused children in the public schools, the only institution that takes them all in.

You want heroes? Visit any special education class and watch the miracle of personal interaction, a job so difficult that fellow teachers are awed by the dedication they witness. There is a sentence from an unnamed source which says, "We have been so anxious to give our children what we didn't have that we have neglected to give them what we did." What is it that our kids really need? What do they really want? Math, science, history and social studies are important, but children need love, confidence, encouragement, someone to talk to, someone to listen, standards to live by. Teachers provide upright examples, the faith and assurance of responsible people.

You want heroes? Then go down to your local school and see our real live heroes—the ones changing lives for the better each and every day!

Now, pass this on to someone you know who's a teacher, or to someone who should thank a teacher today. I'd like to see this sent to all those who cut down the importance of teachers. They have no idea who a public school teacher is or what they do.

Of course we believe this is for all teachers and not just public educators. May the force be with all educators!!

Extreme Teaching for Extreme Times! LLC is dedicated to providing dynamic, engaging, humorous, and innovative best practice strategies aimed at "Teaching to the Heart of the Child". We unequivocally believe that in honoring the hearts of the child, family, and community, "Neither Teacher nor Child Will Be Left Behind". Our goal is to model outrageous joy and servant leadership qualities that have the potential to transform schools in which powerful learning is embraced and celebrated by all.

Target Goals

* Develop exemplary professionals dedicated to greatly increasing student standardized test scores;
* Ignite contagious joy and hope within individual classrooms, schools, and communities;
* Identify, unleash, and celebrate the hidden gifts of staff, parents, students; including those with English as a Second Language;
* Create reflective practitioners whose pedagogical and management strategies are driven by research;
* Assist teachers in forging visions for students and self;
* Strengthen communication, collaboration, and caring among all staff;
* Foster professional learning communities through assertive strategic planning and continuous team building;
* Utilize the "Village" as a wealth of educational resources.

After all...it takes a whole village to prepare a teacher!